— ★ —

PRAISE FOR *TEXAS SLOW COOKER*

"As a fifth generation West Texan, practically raised in a truck-stop cafe, I like to think I know a thing or two about Texas culture and cooking. Much has been written about Texas food over the years, but to my mind no one has quite captured the true essence of the genre like Cheryl Alters Jamison and her late husband Bill Jamison.

I am thrilled that Cheryl is continuing that Texas tradition by herself in this glorious new cookbook. While she updates classic Texas dishes such as King Ranch Chicken Casserole and creates brilliant new ones like Rio Star Grapefruit Pudding Cake, her adaptation and simplification for the slow cooker of the iconic Yucatan dish, Cochinita Pibil, much loved in Texas, is nothing short of brilliant and worth the price of this book alone."

—**Stephan Pyles**, restaurateur, Flora Street Cafe and Stampede 66, Dallas, and cookbook author

"Cheryl Jamison's *Texas Slow Cooker* has inspired us to get 'slow-cooking.' This is a book that helps busy families with crazy schedules to gather round the table and enjoy a home-cooked meal basically stress-free."

—**Lisa and Tom Perini**, Perini Ranch Steakhouse, Buffalo Gap, Texas

"Cheryl Jamison brings her love of Texas cooking to busy kitchens via the slow cooker. Brilliant!"

—**Dotty Griffith**, author of *The Ultimate Tortilla Press Cookbook* and *The Texas Holiday Cookbook*

"With recipes for classic beef enchiladas and King ranch chicken casserole—plus peach cobbler and chocolate sheet cake, two of my favorites—Cheryl Jamison has captured the spirit of Texas cooking, dialed it down to low and slow, and woven it into a book that celebrates the cuisine of our great state."

—**Ellise Pierce**, author of *Cowgirl Chef: Texas Cooking with a French Accent*

— ★ —

TEXAS
SLOW COOKER

125 RECIPES
for the
Lone Star State's
Very Best Dishes,
All Slow-Cooked
to Perfection

CHERYL ALTERS JAMISON

HARVARD COMMON PRESS

Inspiring | Educating | Creating | Entertaining

Brimming with creative inspiration, how-to projects, and useful information to enrich your everyday life, Quarto Knows is a favorite destination for those pursuing their interests and passions. Visit our site and dig deeper with our books into your area of interest: Quarto Creates, Quarto Cooks, Quarto Homes, Quarto Lives, Quarto Drives, Quarto Explores, Quarto Gifts, or Quarto Kids.

© 2017 Quarto Publishing Group USA Inc.
Text © 2017 Cheryl Alters Jamison
Photography © 2017 Quarto Publishing Group USA Inc.

First Published in 2017 by The Harvard Common Press, an imprint of The Quarto Group, 100 Cummings Center, Suite 265-D, Beverly, Massachusetts 01915-6101, USA. T (978) 282-9590 F (978) 283-2742 www.QuartoKnows.com

The Harvard Common Press titles are also available at discount for retail, wholesale, promotional, and bulk purchase. For details, contact the Special Sales Manager by email at specialsales@quarto.com or by mail at The Quarto Group, Attn: Special Sales Manager, 401 Second Avenue North, Suite 310, Minneapolis, MN 55401, USA.

21 20 19 18 17   1 2 3 4 5

ISBN: 978-1-55832-894-5

Digital edition published in 2017

Library of Congress Cataloging-in-Publication Data available

Design: Landers Miller Design
Page Layout: Megan Jones Design
Photography: Glenn Scott Photography
Food and Prop Styling: Natasha St. Hailare Taylor

Printed in China

———⭐———

In memory of Bill—

My Hill Country boy

Wish we'd gotten one more slow dance at Gruene Hall.

———⭐———

CONTENTS

AS THE
BUMPER
STICKER
GOES,
I GOT TO
TEXAS
AS SOON AS
I COULD.

SLOW GOING, TEXAS STYLE: AN INTRODUCTION

I'm not the most likely person to write a book on Texas slow cooking. It's no necessity for me to rely on a cooking method that's more leisurely than a herd of free-range snails. I work at home, so I have the luxury of whipping up lunch or dinner when I wish, easily keeping an eye on a saucepan bubbling away on the stove. I live on my own, making the quantities that are often required in a slow cooker a little hefty. Also, I truly enjoy spending time in the kitchen, playing around with food, rather than simply putting it on and leaving it. I am no fan of many so-called convenience ingredients, ones that are heavily processed, and form the core of so many slow-cooker recipes populating the Internet. Those canned soups, prefab spice blends, and jars of Cheez Whiz don't appeal to me.

So, what brought me to this? I am in awe of a device that encourages and helps families to get a great hot meal on the table, with little hassle. I see how a slow cooker simplifies life for people like my Austin-based daughter, her husband, and their three kids. They have an unending schedule, and slow cooking aids them in sitting down to dinner together many nights of the week. Slow cookers offer another valuable advantage. We all find fast food and other take-out valuable from time to time. However, a cook preparing food at home has total control over how much sugar or sodium goes into a dish. Slow cooking gives busy families a decent shot at having a brief sit-down with the gang to share a good, easy meal between lacrosse, dance class, and theater practice.

I should clarify one other point. Currently, I don't live in Texas. I reside in New Mexico these days, and have for some years. When a major Texas newspaper, a few years ago, wrote a feature story about me and my late husband, Bill, my longtime coauthor, the two of us were described as having a mixed marriage—he was a Texan, I was not.

Texas is, though, under my skin, indelibly and profoundly part of me. As the bumper sticker goes, I got to Texas as soon as I could. Shortly out of college, I moved by choice to Dallas during the go-go era of the late 1970s, and I lived there into the 1980s when a dream arts job lured me to Santa Fe.

Bill's family hails from the Hill Country area, from Buda, Onion Creek, and Sprinkle, all in the Austin area. His grandfather, E.J. Cleveland, is remembered as the first person in Buda to buy a new-fangled automobile, and he was in the Texas State Legislature in the 1930s. Bill lived in Wimberley before coming to

Santa Fe, too, and we returned with frequency to that little charmer of a town on the Blanco River. Over the years, we jumped at opportunities to teach cooking classes at places like the Central Market cooking schools throughout the state, as well as at the Lake Austin Spa, Texas Book Festival, and for super-chef Stephan Pyles. Now on my own, frequent trips take me down through El Paso, the Big Bend area, the Davis Mountains, Buffalo Gap, and to see family in Austin and San Antonio.

Writing together, Bill and I envisioned many of our books—four of which won James Beard Foundation book awards—as paeans to under-recognized or underappreciated topics. Among our early books was *Texas Home Cooking*. Published in 1993, it was among the first in a newer generation of books to recognize and revel in the national cuisine of the Lone Star state. Following it came *Smoke & Spice*, a celebration of American barbecue traditions. It grew organically out of the Texas book and a chance meeting with a founder of Pitts & Spitts, a premiere Houston crafter of barbecue pits meant to last a lifetime and beyond. The craft of smoke cooking was in danger of becoming a lost art when we penned the book. I know that's darned hard to imagine now, with the passion for barbecue that has swept the country and has been taken up by many serious chefs.

No one can possibly think that slow-cooker cooking is endangered. It's never been more popular than it is right now. Heck, people reportedly own more slow cookers than coffee makers. The slow-cooker does, though, have a bit of an image problem, and I think it's a bit undervalued. Lots of folks who are serious cooks, chefs, and culinary professionals are in awe of their fancy *sous vide* machines for cooking very low and slow, but they look down on the accessible home cook's device, the slow cooker. It makes me want to do a slow burn.

A little of that attitude may come from early experiences with a slow cooker, especially for those of us who came of age with slow cookers from a generation ago. We plopped a pile of ingredients into it, set it, and forgot it for thirteen hours. Then we found a pot full of, well, "gray meat and grayer carrots," as one of my colleagues put it recently. Another friend who had experimented with a slow cooker said that no matter what she put in, at the end of the day, everything looked and tasted like beef stew. This book will help you avoid those problems. I've taken the guesswork out of timing, and I've enlivened the recipes and their preparations with seasonings and techniques that I hope will delight all manner of taste buds.

Bold Texas flavors make that part easy. The assertive seasonings common to the state make the perfect recipe for a blended, multicultural pot. It's an interdenominational, homey cooking style of South meets West—where a part of the state sits at the corner of old and New Mexico, where Germans and Czechs set down roots in the nineteenth century, and where they were joined by Vietnamese and Pakistanis in the twentieth century.

What passes, though, for assertive seasonings in other styles of cooking isn't perfect for the slow cooker. The cooking process can rob spices of their punch, making them more like, in the words of iconic Texas politico Jim Hightower, "weaker than Canadian hot sauce." A classic chili recipe, for instance, might call for two garlic cloves, but here I suggest an eyebrow-raising eight to ten cloves. You will see an occasional ingredient that might strike you as odd, for instance soy sauce in a Tex-Mex beef preparation. Soy sauce gives umami-style depth to dishes, which is a particular help with long-cooked dishes. So does Maggi seasoning sauce, a vegetable protein–based sauce with a similar roasty, toasty taste that's great for rounding out sauces, soups, and stews, in particular. Maggi has no soy, but it does have MSG. It is considered essential in the Mexican pantry as well as in Vietnam and other parts of Asia. Sometimes a bit of tomato paste gives the desired depth. When the cooking time is relatively short, I usually sauté the dish's primary spices in oil to start. The process allows their flavors to bloom more fully.

Slow cooking keeps food moist, more so than just about any other technique. Even when meats shed, say, a cup of liquid while cooking down, they do not become dry or leathery. Just about anything you would usually braise can be prepared in a slow cooker, though you can generally cut back on the amount of liquid by 50 percent because there is very minimal evaporation. Many foods you are used to cooking in other ways, like fajitas, can work slow and low, too.

Maybe, on second thought, it's not so unusual for me to write about slow-cooker cooking. I am known for writing about barbecue, the ultimate low-and-slow cooking form, where tough cuts of beef become tender as the connective tissue breaks down. As it happened, I found that some of the techniques I know from the barbecue world actually translate well here. For instance, turbinado sugar—a granular brown sugar—doesn't break down nearly as fast during hours of cooking as more finely processed and ground sugar. The heftier dose of dried spices used in dry rubs, or garlic, for example, in a seasoning paste, help flavor these long-cooked items, too.

And just one more thing. Anyone who has ever sweated his or her way through a blistering Texas summer should welcome a cooking technique that doesn't raise the temperature in the kitchen.

EQUIPMENT FOR SLOWPOKES

In the 1970s, I was gifted a burnt-orange Crock-Pot, one of the models that was made in one piece, making it awkward to wash out. Today, virtually all slow cookers have a removable insert of stoneware or heavy metal that can be removed from the base and washed in a dishwasher. The lids, too, are dishwasher safe. Some lids are hinged, which takes care of the issue of where to set the lid when serving from one of the cookers. If you have a small kitchen, like me, that's quite a helpful feature.

Today's cookers often sport a chrome or stainless steel exterior, or they may be enveloped in another metallic finish, perhaps copper, red, or even purple. Some have a removable exterior wrap, so that the color or pattern can be switched out, depending on your whim or holiday. You can get one emblazoned with the logo of your preferred college or NFL team, or perhaps one with a lid that snaps into place to make it a breeze to tote, perfect for tailgating. If you go to eBay, you might be able to score a model shaped like a football. You can find a Crock-Pot called the Little Dipper, perfect for queso for your tortilla chips, and you can find one large enough to cook an entire turkey.

In the course of writing this book, I have tried out a multitude of slow cookers. Initially, I tested them side-by-side to see if they would come to a boil, or come to another temperature and hold it there. That was pretty much the case. The ones I used most for this book were two models of Crock-Pot. One is a basic round 4- to 5-quart (3.8- to 4.7-l) version, which cost me under twenty dollars at Target. The other is a mid-range, moderately equipped, digital countdown model. Its oval shape holds 6 quarts (5.7 l), and it cost about sixty dollars. The basic model just has a low and high setting. Two helpful features—a timer and a warming setting—come on the pricier version.

My third go-to cooker is a sleek 6-quart (5.7-l) All-Clad, an investment of more than two hundred dollars for a fairly top-of-the-line version, at least when I acquired it. A feature I especially like is that the cooking insert is not ceramic, therefore I worry less about chipping or cracking it when moving around the kitchen. However, given the price difference between it and some other models with ceramic inserts, I could afford

LOTS OF FOLKS WHO ARE SERIOUS COOKS, CHEFS, AND CULINARY PROFESSIONALS ARE IN AWE OF THEIR FANCY *SOUS VIDE* MACHINES FOR COOKING VERY LOW AND SLOW, BUT THEY LOOK DOWN ON THE ACCESSIBLE HOME COOK'S DEVICE, THE SLOW COOKER. IT MAKES ME WANT TO DO A SLOW BURN.

to break several crocks before the cost invested would catch up. Also, the All-Clad features a pair of holes in the lid which vent a bit of excess steam. I find that especially useful when baking something, such as a cake or brownies, in the slow cooker.

The contemporary slow cooker tends to run a bit hotter—on both low and high settings—than the earliest models. This has addressed concerns about keeping the food temperature in the safe range above 140°F (60°C). That means the timing suggested in recipes can and should be more precise than eight to twelve hours, for example.

Today there are slow cookers with a searing plate, and food can be browned off right in the slow cooker, rather than transferred from a skillet to the slow cooker. Some slow cookers can morph into steamers or pressure cookers, too. Take a look at the Crock-Pot multicookers or the model that has an auto-stirring feature. One of the newer models of All-Clad cookers holds 7 quarts (6.6 l); it has three slow-cooking settings, a setting for cooking rice, and a programmable twenty-two-hour timer. Oval cookers are now nearly as common as round ones. Hamilton Beach offers a more design-y looking Party Crock, with a cast-iron insert that can go into the oven.

If you are preparing meals for one or two people, smaller cookers are out there, but I find it's nice to have some leftovers. Most dishes that excel in the slow cooker also keep well for another day or more, so why not have some planned leftovers? If you really want to make a fresh dish daily, just for you, the petite 1½-quart (1.4-l) slow cooker is worth having. These are inexpensive enough you can add one to an existing collection of cookers.

If I were going out to buy a single slow cooker today, it would likely be the 6-quart (5.7-l) Crock-Pot Smart Slow Cooker with WeMo, which retails for about $130. WeMo refers to the cooker's Wi-Fi connected smartphone app, allowing the busy cook to adjust the cooking time or temperature when on the go. Crock-Pot owners can take advantage of live chat online now, too. You can even have Crock-Pot–ready meal kits shipped to your door, ready to pop into your slow cooker. You may not want or need all of the bells and whistles, but it's good to know what's available.

TIPS FOR TAKING IT SLOW

Spray the inside of the cooker with cooking spray or smear it with the wrapper of a stick of butter. Either makes cleanup a cinch. You can buy slow-cooker liners in many supermarkets, but I don't think they are all that helpful and they create one more thing that goes to the landfill.

My recipes are written for slow cookers in the 5- to 6-quart (4.7- to 5.7-l) range. If yours is a 4-quart (3.8-l) model, you can make minor adjustments such as using a 2½-pound (1.1-kg) roast rather than the called-for 3-pound (1.4-kg) one. Subtract one red waxy potato, for instance, or ½ cup (120 ml) from the main source of liquid. If you have a 7-quart (6.6-l) big-boy slow cooker, you can opt for up to a ½ pound (225 g) more meat or poultry, or add a couple of carrots, another chunk of onion, and another potato, to bulk up the ingredients. The suggested cooking times won't be far off the mark.

Some dishes, like an omelet or brownies, can be presented more attractively when removed from the slow cooker whole or intact. An insert of crisscross pieces of aluminum foil—a sling of sorts—can be molded to the inside of the slow cooker before adding the food, and then used to lift out the finished dish when ready.

I recommend a quartet of easy-to-find kitchen equipment if you want to take advantage of every recipe here. You may already have them in your home cabinets. One is a high-sided quart (946 ml) soufflé dish; another is a 6-inch (15-cm) cake pan with a 2-inch (5-cm) tall rim; another is a 6-inch (15-cm) springform pan, the kind used for cheesecake. All come in handy when baking in the slow cooker. The last item is a round metal biscuit cutter, about 3 inches (7.5 cm) in diameter. You'll be using it "off label," in this case. It makes a perfect stand for any of the dishes or pans you want to lift from the bottom of the slow cooker, balancing them well.

Vegetables cook more slowly than meat. To counter this, I suggest putting dense vegetables such as carrots and potatoes at the bottom of the slow cooker or along its edge, closer to the heating element. You can also cut those vegetables in smaller chunks than the meat, in a dish like a stew, for instance.

In general, fill slow cookers approximately three-fourths full. I have to admit I ignore this routinely with smaller quantities, and they just cook a little faster. If your food quantity is really light though, add some more vegetables to bulk up the quantity. Don't go over three-quarters full

ANYONE WHO HAS EVER SWEATED HIS OR HER WAY THROUGH A BLISTERING TEXAS SUMMER SHOULD WELCOME A COOKING TECHNIQUE THAT DOESN'T RAISE THE TEMPERATURE IN THE KITCHEN.

though because hot ingredients can expand. The exception to that rule is with greens, where they wilt and cook down substantially.

Even on low heat, the exterior of every slow cooker I have worked with gets hot, as does the lid. From my experience, even handles that look like they are meant to be heatproof get uncomfortably warm. Make sure everyone working or playing in your kitchen knows this. Keep the slow cooker back from the edge of the counter and the cooker's cord safely tucked behind it.

One of the advantages of a slow cooker is the ability to leave it all day, almost always on the low setting. Since the heat radiates from the sides, make sure the cooker is on a heatproof surface, and pulled away from walls and cabinets. Vent holes in the lid should be free to let steam out into the air, rather than into the bottom of a cabinet.

Avoid opening the cooker more than absolutely necessary. It's not just that you let out the slowly built-up warmth. The steam created forms a seal around the edge of the lid. It's broken when opened, and then needs to form again when the lid is replaced.

The high setting cooks about twice as fast as the low. Each cooker works just a bit differently than all of the others. The first time you try a recipe, check a little in advance of the time projected for doneness. Make notes on the recipes as you complete them in case you need a small adjustment. It will likely always require the same adjustment whenever you prepare it in the future.

Every recipe notes the expected number of hours required for cooking each dish. If the cooking time on high is mentioned first, that's the preferred heat level, but the other works nearly as well. If a recipe only lists "on high" or "on low," it's because you don't get the desired result using the other setting. For example, most of the dessert recipes are cooked exclusively on high. For your convenience, I also have noted when a recipe can be held in the slow cooker on "warm" without compromising its texture or taste.

Avoid putting a hot crock in a sink of cold water or running cold water into it. Be careful, too, with icy granite counters on a winter morning or in the height of air conditioning season.

Don't put a heated slow cooker insert filled with food into the refrigerator. It won't cool quickly enough to avoid the danger zone for bacteria. It's okay though to prepare a crock with a recipe and refrigerate it overnight, for example. Let it come to room temperature before proceeding. Never start a recipe with a block of frozen food.

Most digital slow cookers have a warm mode to keep food that way for up to several hours after cooking. They won't allow you to put food in and then have a delayed start because of safety concerns. Never use the warm setting to slow down the cooking. It's too low a temperature to cook safely.

Part of slow-cooker culture has been the heavy reliance on processed ingredients, whether canned soups or sawdust-tasting, prefab seasonings. I can appreciate that speed is integral to getting the food into the pot. I use a few canned or jarred items, ones that I find of good quality, especially canned broth and tomato products. I also like Ro-Tel–style tomatoes and green chiles, and evaporated milk for making sauces that don't break during extra-long cooking. I would much rather, though, measure out the ingredients needed for a dry seasoning blend instead of ripping open a packet of stale dry rub or taco seasoning made mostly of salt and sugar.

Today's Texas cooking uses a generous amount of long green chiles from neighboring New Mexico, often called Hatch chiles in popular late summer and fall promotions. There isn't actually a Hatch variety, but use them and enjoy them, whatever you call them. Find them fresh in late summer and fall; at other times during the year, look for frozen versions, such as Bueno Foods, or jarred versions, such as 505 Southwestern brand.

If you prepare food at an especially high altitude, the boiling temperature of liquid lowers. That means it takes longer for foods to cook. I have tested recipes near sea level and up to 7,000 feet altitude, and I have found the differences in the approximate time range already common to slow cooking to be minimal. The one exception is dried beans. They may indeed take up to several more hours than mentioned, and they may need more liquid added to avoid drying out.

SURE WAYS TO LIVEN UP SLOW FOODS

Foods that come out of a slow cooker sometimes suffer from the moosh texture. I have tried to avoid that in the basic structure and timing of my recipes as much as possible. There are many little hacks you can use to add contrasting crunch or crispness or brightness:

- Toasted bread crumbs, small panko type crumbs, or torn, larger, uneven bits of country bread toasted in a skillet with butter or oil.

- Finely chopped herbs with lemon, lime, orange, or tangerine zest. Add a little garlic or onion, if you wish.

- Citrus juice or zest.

- Watercress or arugula leaves, maybe with a touch of oil-and-vinegar dressing.

- Pumpkin seeds, sunflower kernels, black or white sesame seeds, or chopped or slivered nuts.

- French-fried onion rings. Yes, those cans of the holiday's favorite casserole topping. Make something similar if you like, from scratch, by frying thinly sliced shallots in about an inch (2.5 cm) of vegetable oil until they crisp.

- *Chicharrónes*, or fried pork rinds, chopped in a food processor or blender.

- Grated or spiralized carrots, cucumbers, or zucchini.

- Slivered snow peas or other fresh vegetables.

- Simple quick-pickled vegetables, such as cucumbers, carrots, jalapeños, or jicama. To 1 cup (235 ml) each of vinegar and sugar, add 2 to 3 teaspoons (12 to 18 g) of salt, and refrigerate for at least several hours.

- Fermented escabeche (jalapeños, carrots, and onions) or sauerkraut or other pickles, chopped if needed.

- Pico de gallo or other fresh salsa, or chowchow or other vegetable relish.

- Quick, simple, shredded cabbage salad, with splashes of oil and vinegar, and sprinklings of salt and pepper.

- Salad of tiny homegrown tomatoes or farmers' market tomatoes, halved and tossed with enough oil to glisten, and a generous dusting of salt and pepper.

- Chopped store-bought pickled okra or pickled watermelon rind.

A quick history of slow cooking includes the fact that Joe Garagiola, genial Major League Baseball catcher, broadcaster, and NBC *Today* show regular, was enlisted for a 1970s ad campaign for Rival's Crock-Pot. What a knock-it-out-of-the-ballpark success the slow cooker has become. Enjoy using yours, along with this book, for a celebration of Texas tastes.

A BREAKFAST TO KICKSTART YOUR DAY

OATMEAL WITH CRUNCHY PECANS

YIELD: SERVES 4 | COOKING TIME: 6 TO 7 HOURS ON LOW, CAN BE HELD ON WARM UP TO 2 HOURS

I'll bet some of you know there's an Oatmeal, Texas . . . but how about Coffee and Coffee City? Ponder that over breakfast, but keep in mind too that there's a Ponder, Texas. On to the recipe at hand, though, which is something of an overnight sensation. The best way to make really high-quality oatmeal is actually while you sleep. If you love figs, add several chopped dried figs to the mixture before cooking.

1 teaspoon unsalted butter

1 cup (120 g) steel-cut oats

2 cups (470 ml) whole milk

2 cups (470 ml) water

3 tablespoons (60 g) maple syrup, agave nectar, or packed brown sugar

½ teaspoon salt

½ cup (55 g) chopped pecans, toasted in a dry skillet until fragrant

Maple syrup or agave nectar, optional

Milk or cream, optional

① Generously grease the inside of the slow cooker with butter.

② Add the oats, milk, water, maple syrup, and salt to the slow cooker, and stir together. Scatter pecans over the oat mixture. Cover and cook on the low heat setting for 6 to 7 hours until the oats are creamy. The pecans will be a bit more crisp and brown, too.

③ Spoon into bowls and serve hot. If you wish, top the oatmeal with maple syrup or agave nectar, or with a couple of spoonfuls of milk or cream.

OVERNIGHT GRITS

YIELD: SERVES 4 TO 6 | **COOKING TIME:** 7 TO 8 HOURS ON LOW, CAN BE HELD ON WARM FOR 1 HOUR

Here's another way to make food while you sleep. Make sure you have whole-grain corn grits, not instant grits. Serve with breakfast sausage, sautéed trout fillets, or poached or fried eggs. I like putting together a layered parfait version of the grits, with alternating layers of crumbled sautéed sausage, grated Cheddar, and maybe some cooked mustard greens, chard, or other dark leafy greens.

1 teaspoon unsalted butter

3 cups (705 ml) water

¾ cup (117 g) corn grits

3 ounces (85 g) cream cheese, cut in bits

1 teaspoon kosher salt or coarse sea salt

½ teaspoon Tabasco sauce or other tangy hot sauce, or more to taste

① Generously grease the inside of the slow cooker with butter.

② Combine all of the ingredients in the slow cooker. Cover and cook on the low heat setting for about 7 hours, or until the grits are creamy. Spoon onto plates or into bowls.

③ Leftover grits can be spooned into a greased baking dish, then covered and refrigerated. Once firm, the grits can be cut into squares and fried in butter on a griddle or in a skillet until lightly browned and crispy on the surface.

CRUNCHY PECAN-AND-POPPY SEED FRENCH TOAST CASSEROLE

YIELD: SERVES 6 TO 8 | COOKING TIME: 2 TO 2½ HOURS ON HIGH

So much of the enjoyment of food is—or should be—about texture. One of the tricks I learned while writing about barbecue is that coarse turbinado sugar doesn't melt into dishes with the speed of more finely ground sugars. You can use that characteristic to your advantage here, sprinkling part of it over the top of the French toast. The crunch is magnified by the generous use of pecans and poppy seeds. This makes a scrumptious Sunday supper as well as a late weekend breakfast or brunch. You can assemble the ingredients in the insert of the slow cooker and refrigerate overnight to speed things in the morning, if you wish.

1 teaspoon unsalted butter

1 pound (455 g) day-old challah, brioche, or soft thin-crusted white bread, in 1½- to 2-inch (1- to 5-cm) cubes

½ cup (55 g) chopped pecans

2 teaspoons (6 g) poppy seeds

2 cups (470 ml) half-and-half

1 cup (235 ml) whole milk

4 large eggs plus 2 additional egg yolks

½ cup (200 g) turbinado sugar (divided)

2 teaspoons (10 ml) pure vanilla extract

¼ teaspoon ground cinnamon

¼ teaspoon kosher salt or coarse sea salt

Softened unsalted butter or warm maple syrup (or both), for accompaniment

① Generously grease the inside of the slow cooker with butter.

② Place the bread cubes in the slow cooker. Scatter the pecans and poppy seeds over and around the bread.

③ Whisk together in a bowl the half-and-half, milk, eggs and yolks, all but 2 tablespoons (50 g) of the sugar, the vanilla, cinnamon, and salt. Pour the mixture over the bread. Push the bread back down into the half-and-half mixture. (The mixture can be prepared to this point and refrigerated overnight. It will add a few minutes to the cooking time.) Sprinkle the remaining 2 tablespoons (50 g) of sugar over the casserole.

④ Cover and cook on the high heat setting for 2 to 2½ hours. The French toast is ready when the custard mixture is creamy, lightly set, and a bit puffy. Uncover and let sit for 15 minutes.

⑤ Spoon the French toast out onto plates and top, if you wish, with butter or syrup or both. I don't think it needs a thing, but go with your desires. Serve right away.

PUFFY GERMAN APPLE PANCAKE

YIELD: SERVES 4 | COOKING TIME: 2 TO 2½ HOURS ON LOW

The custard-y pancake stays creamier in the slow cooker than it does when oven-baked in conventional fashion in a cast-iron skillet. The apples will float upward, which will lace the pancake with more of their flavor than the skillet-cooked version of this dish. If you want to change up the flavor profile a bit, substitute nutmeg for the cinnamon and add ½ teaspoon of ground powdered ginger when the portion of nutmeg is added to the batter.

4 tablespoons (½ stick, or 55 g) unsalted butter (divided)

2 large tangy apples, such as Granny Smith, peeled and sliced

½ cup (115 g) packed brown sugar

1 teaspoon ground cinnamon (divided)

¾ cup (94 g) unbleached all-purpose flour

⅓ cup (66 g) granulated sugar

½ teaspoon kosher salt or coarse sea salt

1¼ cups (295 ml) whole milk

4 large eggs

½ teaspoon pure vanilla extract

Maple syrup or sour cream (or both), optional

① Generously grease the inside of the slow cooker with 1 teaspoon of the butter.

② Melt the remaining butter in a large skillet over medium heat. Stir in the apples and cook 3 to 4 minutes, until somewhat softened. Scatter the brown sugar and ½ teaspoon cinnamon over the apples and continue cooking for another minute, until the sugar melts and mixture is bubbly. Scrape the apple mixture into the slow cooker.

③ Whisk together in a medium bowl the flour, sugar, salt, and remaining ½ teaspoon cinnamon. Whisk in the milk. Add the eggs and vanilla, and whisk until well combined. Eliminate any lumps with the side of the whisk. Pour the mixture over the apples.

④ Cover and cook on the low heat setting for 2 to 2½ hours, or until the pancake is puffed and no longer jiggly in the center. Poke the pancake with a knife to make sure that the mixture is no longer runny.

⑤ Let the pancake sit uncovered in the slow cooker for up to 30 minutes. Serve by scooping up (go all the way to the bottom) portions neatly and plating them. If you wish, serve with maple syrup, sour cream, or both.

FRITOS-CRUSTED CORN QUICHE

YIELD: SERVES 6 OR MORE | COOKING TIME: 1½ TO 2¼ HOURS ON HIGH, PLUS 15 TO 30 MINUTES STANDING TIME

I pondered the inclusion of a breakfast dish made with Fritos, the iconic invented-in-Texas staple. Some folks might look askance on the tasty-but-prefab chips as morning food. Then I figured there'd be other folks who might harrumph that no true Texan would eat quiche at daybreak. What trumped those concerns was the taste, and the truly proudly Texan story behind the Fritos folks, the Doolin family. Their small San Antonio confectionary grew into the Frito-Lay corporation. I modified a recipe found in *Fritos Pie*, a fun little book penned by Kaleta Doolin, daughter of the company founder.

Vegetable oil spray

2 cups (75 g) Fritos corn chips

1 tablespoon (14 g) unsalted butter, melted

1 cup (120 g) grated mild cheddar cheese (divided)

1 tablespoon (14 g) unsalted butter

1 cup (164 g) corn kernels, fresh or frozen

⅓ cup (55 g) diced sweet onion, such as Texas 1015, or red onion

⅓ cup (50 g) diced red bell pepper

3 large eggs

1 cup (235 ml) half-and-half

¾ teaspoon kosher salt or coarse sea salt

① Spray the interior of a 6-inch (15-cm) springform pan with oil and, unless you know it is leakproof, wrap aluminum foil around the exterior tightly.

② In a food processor, make crumbs of the Fritos. Pour in the butter and pulse another time or two to combine. Pour the crumb mixture into the pan and press into an even layer. Scatter two-thirds (80 g) of the filling's cheese over the crust.

③ In a skillet, warm the butter over medium heat. Add the corn, onion, and bell pepper, and sauté until the vegetables are just tender. Spoon the mixture evenly into the crust.

④ In a bowl, whisk together the eggs, half-and-half, and salt. Pour the custard over the other ingredients in the pan. Top with the rest of the cheese.

⑤ Place the pan in the slow cooker and cover. Cook on high for 1½ to 2 hours, until the quiche is lightly set but is still moist looking. Turn off the slow cooker and let the quiche sit in it uncovered for about 15 minutes. Transfer to a work surface. Run a knife between the quiche and the springform pan. Remove the pan. Slice the quiche, and serve warm or at room temperature. Refrigerate any leftovers.

OPEN-FACE OMELET WITH SAUSAGE AND HOME FRIES

YIELD: SERVES 6 OR MORE | COOKING TIME: 3½ TO 4 HOURS ON LOW

This frittata's a hearty—but not overly heavy—way to start the day.

2 tablespoons (30 ml) olive oil

8 ounces (225 g) well-seasoned bulk breakfast sausage

12 ounces (340 g) russet potato, peeled and cut in ⅓-inch (9-mm) dice

1 handful fresh spinach leaves, chopped coarse, optional

1 teaspoon kosher salt or coarse sea salt

Freshly ground black pepper

10 large eggs

① Generously grease the inside of the slow cooker with about 1 teaspoon of the oil. Line the slow cooker with 2 pieces of aluminum foil, at least 12 inches (30 cm) in length each, arranged in crisscross directions.

② Warm the remaining oil in a skillet over medium heat and add the sausage to it. Spoon out the sausage onto a plate. Add the potatoes to the sausage drippings and sauté until almost tender, about 10 minutes. If using the spinach, add it and cook briefly, until it wilts and any liquid has evaporated. Stir in the salt and several hearty grindings of pepper.

③ Transfer the mixture to the slow cooker, smoothing the surface. Whisk together the eggs in a bowl, then pour them over the sausage mixture. If the foil extends beyond the top edge of the slow cooker, fold it in. Cover and cook until the omelet's center is just set, 3½ to 4 hours on the low heat setting.

④ Let the omelet sit in the uncovered slow cooker for 10 to 15 minutes. Using the foil for support, transfer the omelet to a cutting board or platter. Peel the foil away. Slice the omelet and serve.

CHILE RELLENO CASSEROLE

YIELD: SERVES 6 | COOKING TIME: 6 TO 7 HOURS ON LOW

Individually filled and fried chiles rellenos are usually a dish for lunch or dinner.
However, this casserole version makes a fine morning eye-opener. Long, green, New Mexican chiles are
sometimes incorrectly called Anaheims, and they are often known in Texas as Hatch chiles, after the
New Mexico town close to a large part of the legendary green chile harvest.

Vegetable oil spray

6 large fresh mild-to-medium
New Mexican green chiles,
roasted and peeled

½ cup (64 g) unbleached
all-purpose flour

1 teaspoon kosher salt or coarse
sea salt

¾ cup (175 ml) half-and-half

4 large eggs

1¼ cups (150 g) shredded medium
Cheddar or Colby cheese (divided)

1 cup (115 g) shredded Jack cheese

Your favorite tomato or tomatillo salsa

1. Generously spray the inside of the slow cooker with oil.

2. Slice the chiles down the side, scrape out the seeds, and cut off the stems. Cut each chile into about 6 lengthwise strips.

3. Whisk together in a medium bowl the flour and salt, then add the half-and-half, and then add the eggs. Whisk until smooth.

4. Combine 1 cup (120 g) of the Cheddar cheese with the Jack cheese. Make two or three layers of the chiles and cheese. Two layers will likely work best in an oval slow cooker, three if the cooker is round. Lay out chile strips side-by-side for each layer, then scatter with cheese. Pour the batter over the top, covering the mixture.

5. Cover and cook on the low heat setting for 6 to 7 hours until batter is set. Scoop individual servings out with a large spoon and serve with salsa.

STRATA WITH CHORIZO AND PEPPERS

YIELD: SERVES 6 TO 8 | COOKING TIME: 3½ TO 4 HOURS ON LOW

Stratas are my go-to breakfast or brunch entertaining solutions. Often, these are just referred to as overnight casseroles because they are typically best assembled early so that the bread can absorb all of the creamy, dreamy custard. However, the low slow cooking here gives enough time for the bread to soak up the mixture so it's not necessary to make ahead. You can, though, if it helps get it on the table when you wish. Presuming your slow cooker has a removable insert, you can assemble the strata the night before you plan to serve it. In the morning, let it sit at room temperature long enough to take the chill off the crock. Then give it an additional 30 minutes or so of cooking time. Tomatoes would be a good addition to the chorizo mixture if in season, or halved cherry tomatoes could be served over individual servings of the strata.

Vegetable oil spray

8 ounces (225 g) bulk chorizo or other spicy bulk sausage

1 red bell pepper, chopped

1 green bell pepper, chopped

3 garlic cloves, minced

½ teaspoon Maggi sauce or soy sauce (divided)

1-pound (455-g) loaf country or sourdough bread, crusts removed if thick

1½ cups (172 g) Monterey Jack or Muenster cheese, grated

1 cup (225 g) small-curd cottage cheese or farmer's cheese

6 large eggs

1 cup (235 ml) whole milk

1 teaspoon dry mustard

¾ teaspoon kosher salt or coarse sea salt

Freshly ground black pepper

1. Generously spray the inside of the slow cooker with oil. Line it with 2 pieces of aluminum foil, at least 12 inches (30 cm) in length each, arranged in the slow cooker in crisscross directions.

2. Sauté the chorizo in a skillet over medium heat until it has cooked through, about 10 minutes. Add the bell peppers and garlic to the pan, and cook until the peppers are tender, about 5 more minutes. Stir in ¼ teaspoon of the Maggi sauce.

3. Slice the bread into 9 to 12 slices no more than ½ inch (1 cm) thick. Arrange the bread (tearing some of the slices if needed to fit the shape of the slow cooker), cheese, cottage cheese, and the chorizo mixture in three equal alternating layers.

4. Whisk the eggs with the milk, mustard, salt, pepper, and remaining ¼ teaspoon of Maggi sauce. Pour the custard evenly over the bread mixture. Press down on the bread, if needed to submerge it. If the foil extends beyond the top edge of the slow cooker, fold it in. Cover and cook until the strata is lightly set at the center, 3½ to 4 hours on the low heat setting.

5. Uncover and let the strata cool in the slow cooker for about 15 minutes. Using the foil to lift the strata, remove it from the slow cooker. Spoon onto plates and serve hot.

POACHED EGGS

YIELD: Serving size varies | COOKING TIME: About 45 minutes

For huevos rancheros, any form of Benedict, or perhaps poached eggs on Texas toast or English muffins, you can make a foolproof collection of poached eggs simultaneously. Figure out the maximum number of 3-inch (7.5-cm) ramekins you can fit in your slow cooker, then decide if you want to make that many or something less. These are technically coddled eggs because they are cooked in ramekins in the water. Poached eggs are more correctly cracked directly into water, but the results are pretty much identical otherwise.

Vegetable oil spray

Large eggs, preferably from a farmers' market or other fresh source

Kosher salt or coarse sea salt

Freshly ground black pepper

Splash of any hot sauce, optional

1. Arrange the number of ramekins you intend to use in the slow cooker. Add enough hot water to come up to the middle of the ramekins. Remove the ramekins and set on a convenient counter. Cover the slow cooker and let it heat the water on the high setting for 30 minutes.

2. While the water heats, spray each ramekin with oil. Crack an egg into each ramekin and sprinkle with salt and pepper and, if you wish, hot sauce.

3. Transfer the ramekins back to the slow cooker. For poached eggs with a viscous but runny center, about 15 minutes should give you a perfect quivering result. If you have people who get queasy about a runny yolk, roll your eyes, and cook their eggs for about 5 more minutes.

4. Remove immediately from the slow cooker and spoon out onto plates as you wish to serve them. Eat right away.

MENUDO

YIELD: SERVES 6 TO 8 | COOKING TIME: 8 TO 9 HOURS ON LOW, CAN BE HELD ON WARM FOR 2 HOURS

Considered the ultimate hangover cure, menudo migrated up from Sonora. You'll have no trouble finding tripe in any Mexican market. Pick up the ham hock or other pork for the recipe there, too.

2 pounds (905 g) cleaned honeycomb tripe, in bite-size pieces

Vegetable oil spray

1 smoked ham hock, pig's foot, or pork knuckle

2 medium onions, chopped

6 garlic cloves, minced

2 to 4 fresh serrano chiles, minced

2 tablespoons (15 g) chili powder

1 tablespoon (3 g) crumbled dried Mexican oregano or marjoram

½ teaspoon coarse-ground black pepper

4 cups (940 ml) low-sodium chicken broth

1 can (14½ to 16 ounces, 411 to 455 g) hominy, drained

Kosher salt or coarse sea salt

Lime wedges, for garnish

Chopped fresh cilantro or fresh mint, for garnish

① Place the tripe in a saucepan and cover it with cold water. Bring to a rapid boil over high heat, and boil for 30 minutes. Drain the tripe. (This step can be done a day ahead, if you wish. Refrigerate covered until needed.)

② Generously spray the inside of the slow cooker with oil.

③ Combine in the cooker the tripe, ham hock, onions, garlic, serranos, chili powder, oregano, black pepper, and broth. Cook on the low heat setting for 8 to 9 hours. Remove the ham hock and shred its meat, discarding any fat or bone. Return the ham hock meat to the cooker, add the hominy, and salt to taste. Heat through about 30 minutes more. The tripe should be tender though it will still have a touch of chewiness.

④ Spoon the menudo into large bowls and serve steaming with your choice of lime, cilantro, or mint, or a combination of all the garnishes.

STARTERS, TAILGATING SNACKS, AND SOUPS

QUESO

YIELD: SERVES 6 TO 8 | COOKING TIME: 1½ HOUR ON LOW, CAN BE HELD FOR 2 HOURS ON WARM

"A Texan's sixth food group," proclaimed *Texas Monthly* magazine about queso. That begs the question of what items could possibly rank as items one through five. You simply need a go-to queso for game day, whether tailgating or watching on TV, and for every other gathering of three or more. I can't arrive in Austin to visit family without an immediate trip to Torchy's Tacos, home of my gold standard for store-bought queso. A slow cooker makes one of the best serving dishes for this bubbling, molten, cheese blend. Queso can be as simple as a melded block of Velveeta and can of Ro-Tel tomatoes and green chiles. Even that can seduce someone with food pretensions. This version ups the flavor complexity a bit without adding too much work to the process. American cheese is still processed but, at least to me, has a bit more real cheese character than Velveeta. This may not be Torchy's, but it sure is good.

1 teaspoon unsalted butter

¼ cup (36 g) minced seeded fresh jalapeño

12 ounces (340 g) American cheese, in ¾-inch (2-cm) dice (If sliced, stack up about half of the slices and cut into blocks, then repeat.)

3 ounces (85 g) cream cheese, in ¾-inch (2-cm) dice

1 teaspoon granulated garlic

1 can (10 ounces, or 280 g) tomatoes and green chiles, such as Ro-Tel

1 tablespoon (8g) cornstarch

½ cup (120 ml) low-sodium chicken or vegetable broth

Tortilla chips

① Generously grease the inside of the slow cooker with butter.

② Scatter jalapeño in the bottom of the slow cooker, then add the cheeses, garlic, and tomatoes and green chiles. In a small bowl, stir together the cornstarch with several tablespoons of the broth. Pour it and the rest of the broth into the slow cooker.

③ Cook on the low heat setting for 1½ hours, or until fully melted. Stir as needed to combine. Serve the queso from the slow cooker, or spoon out into small bowls while the rest stays warm. In either case, serve with tortilla chips.

⋈ BOB ARMSTRONG DIP ⋈

Named after the former Texas Land Commissioner and not the WWE wrestler, "Bob" dip is a menu item from Matt's El Rancho in Austin, originally. To make a version of it, layer warm Picadillo San Antonio Sister-in-Law Style (page 82), topped by a similar amount of queso, then add a scoop of guacamole and sour cream, and serve with tortilla chips.

JALAPEÑO SPINACH-ARTICHOKE DIP

YIELD: SERVES 6 | COOKING TIME: 1 TO 1½ HOURS ON HIGH, 2 TO 3 HOURS ON LOW

Sure, spinach-artichoke dips are ubiquitous, but that's because they taste so good. This one's fired up with a hit of pickled jalapeño and, of course, served warm from its cooking. Results for this creamy dip are best when it is made in a quart (946 ml) soufflé dish or other bake-proof dish set inside the slow cooker with a water bath.

Vegetable oil spray

8 ounces (225 g) cream cheese

½ cup (115 g) mayonnaise

1 tablespoon (15 ml) olive oil

2 minced pickled jalapeños, plus
2 tablespoons (28 ml) pickling
liquid from the jar

1 plump garlic clove

¼ teaspoon ground cumin

¼ teaspoon kosher salt or other
coarse salt

1 package (10 ounces, or 280 g) frozen
chopped spinach, thawed, drained,
and squeezed of liquid

1 package (9 to 10 ounces, 255 to
280 g) frozen artichoke hearts,
thawed and chopped

Several grinds of black pepper

Tortilla chips or thin-sliced baguette

① Generously spray the inside of the slow cooker with oil.

② Combine all of the ingredients in a soufflé dish or other bake-proof dish that fits in the slow cooker. It's okay to plop in the entire block of cream cheese. It will all melt down as needed. Place the dish in the slow cooker and pour 1 to 2 cups (235 to 470 ml) of hot water around the outside of the dish. You want it to come up the side of the dish about 1 inch (2.5 cm). Cover and cook on the high setting for 1 to 1½ hours until heated through. Stir together well.

③ Serve hot with tortilla chips.

SEVEN-LAYER DIP

YIELD: SERVES 6 | COOKING TIME: 1 TO 1½ HOURS ON HIGH, 2 TO 3 HOURS ON LOW

A game day classic, you may find your guests tackling each other to finish this off. You can find some two or three zillion versions of this style of dip online, often using unseasoned ground beef as one of the layers. Boring. Chorizo gives a lot more pizzazz. You can argue over what constitutes a layer, and whether there should be things like canned black olives, but if you argue too long, it will all be gone. The presentation is best for this when it is made in a soufflé dish or other bake-proof dish set inside the slow cooker with an added water bath.

Vegetable oil spray

1 can (15 ounces, or 425 g) refried beans or 2 cups homemade refried beans

½ teaspoon ground cumin

1 cup (120 g) grated mild Cheddar cheese

8 ounces (225 g) bulk Mexican-style chorizo, sautéed

1 cup (135 g) mild-to-medium, chopped, roasted New Mexican green chile, juices drained

½ cup (80 g) minced, really minced, red onion

1 cup (230 g) sour cream

1 cup (260 g) tomato or tomatillo salsa

1 cup (115 g) grated Monterey Jack or pepper Jack

Some combination of chopped tomato, canned black olives, pimento-stuffed green olives, or scallions, for garnish

Tortilla chips or Fritos

① Generously spray the inside of the slow cooker with oil.

② Spread the refried beans in the bottom of a soufflé dish or other bake-proof dish that fits in the slow cooker. If the beans are too thick to spread, mix in a bit of water until the consistency is right. Sprinkle cumin over the beans. Add a layer of Cheddar, followed by chorizo, green chile, onion, sour cream, and salsa.

③ Place the dish in the slow cooker and pour 1 to 2 cups (235 to 470 ml) of hot water around the outside of the dish. You want it to come up the side of the dish about 1 inch (2.5 cm). Cover and cook on the high setting for 1 to 1½ hours or on low for 2 to 3 hours, until heated through.

④ Remove the dish from the slow cooker and top with the Monterey Jack cheese, then scatter the top with your choice of garnishes. Serve hot with tortilla chips or Fritos.

SPICY PECANS

YIELD: MAKES 3 CUPS | COOKING TIME: 2 TO 2½ HOURS ON HIGH, CAN BE HELD ON WARM FOR 2 MORE HOURS

You never need to worry about nuts burning when you prepare them in a slow cooker.

2 tablespoons (28 g) unsalted butter, cut in 8 bits

1 pound (455 g) pecan halves

1 tablespoon (8 g) chili powder, or to taste

1 teaspoon granulated sugar

1 teaspoon kosher salt or coarse sea salt, or more to taste

① Generously grease the inside of the slow cooker with about 1 teaspoon of the butter.

② Pour the pecans into the slow cooker. Scatter the remaining butter pieces over the nuts. Sprinkle chili powder, sugar, and salt over all. Cover and cook on the high heat setting for approximately 2 hours. Uncover and stir the nuts well. Cook without the lid for another 15 minutes, or until the nuts have dried out just a bit and have a subtle but distinct crunch.

③ Eat warm or cool. Cover tightly to keep for up to several days.

CHILTEPIN SESAME PEANUTS

YIELD: MAKES 3 CUPS | COOKING TIME: 2 TO 2½ HOURS ON HIGH, CAN BE HELD UP TO 2 HOURS ON WARM

The peanut never seems to get as much love as the pecan, despite Texas's position agriculturally as the second largest producer of the legumes. *Chiltepins*—sometimes called chili tepins—are little, bitty, round, dried chiles that birds seem to love, and because of that, they drop quite a few seeds around for a substantial wild chiltepin population. You can substitute another hot crushed chile, such as what pizza restaurants give you to zip up their pies. I threw in some sesame seeds too, after thinking how good peanuts and sesame can be together in Mexican-inspired mole.

2 tablespoons (30 ml) peanut oil (divided)

1 pound (455 g) shelled unsalted raw peanuts

1 tablespoon (8 g) sesame seeds

2 teaspoons (5 g) crushed dried chiltepin chiles or hot red chile flakes

1 teaspoon kosher salt or coarse sea salt, or to taste

① Generously grease the inside of the slow cooker with about 1 teaspoon of the oil.

② Pour the peanuts and sesame seeds into the slow cooker. Drizzle the remaining oil over the nuts. Sprinkle crushed chiles and salt over all, and stir well. Cover and cook on the high heat setting for approximately 2 hours. Uncover and stir the nuts well. Cook without the lid for another 15 minutes, or until the nuts have dried out just a bit and have a subtle but distinct crunch.

③ Eat warm or cool. Cover tightly to keep for up to several days.

JALA-PEACH WINGS

YIELD: SERVES 6 OR MORE | COOKING TIME: 4 TO 4½ HOURS ON LOW, 2 TO 2½ HOURS ON HIGH

Give your chicken wings a decided Texas kick with a saucy mix of sweet and hot.
Chicken wings need to be browned off to crisp the skin somewhat before going
into the slow cooker. Otherwise, the skin stays flabby and unappealing.

3 tablespoons (42 g) unsalted butter
(divided)

3 pounds (1.4 kg) chicken wings, wing
tips removed, or wing drumettes

1 cup (320 g) peach jam

¼ cup (40 g) minced onion

3 tablespoons (27 g) minced pickled
jalapeño plus 1 tablespoon (15 ml)
pickling liquid from the jar

1 teaspoon Worcestershire sauce

½ teaspoon kosher salt or coarse
sea salt

¼ teaspoon ground cumin

① Generously grease the inside of the slow cooker with about
1 teaspoon of the butter.

② Warm the rest of the butter in a large skillet over medium heat. Sauté
the wings, in batches if needed, until they are nicely colored on all
sides. Transfer the wings to the slow cooker as they are done. When
all wings are browned, add the other ingredients to the slow cooker
and give it all a stir. Cover and cook on the low heat setting for 4 to
4½ hours, or 2 to 2½ hours on high, until the wings are tender and
gooey good.

③ Serve from the slow cooker on the warm setting for a casual event,
or transfer to a plate and serve.

TORTILLA SOUP

YIELD: SERVES 6 TO 8 | COOKING TIME: 5 TO 6 HOURS ON LOW, CAN BE HELD FOR 1 MORE HOUR ON WARM

It has been years since I have been in San Antonio on a Saturday afternoon. That's unfortunate because it's the only time that El Mirador, a restaurant founded by the Trevino family in the late 1960s, serves its steaming bowls of a very special tortilla soup, called *sopa Azteca*. The kitchen there makes it over several days, starting with the simmering of whole chickens, the basis for the rich broth. This is my version for a home cook, which uses the slow cooker to coax out lots of deep chicken goodness. You can make a simpler tortilla soup, but it's hard to make one that's better. This is a full meal in a bowl.

Vegetable oil spray

2 pounds (905 g) ripe plum tomatoes

1 large onion, chunked

6 plump garlic cloves

1 or 2 canned chipotle chiles with 2 teaspoons (10 g) adobo sauce from the can

2 pounds (905 g) bone-in skin-on chicken thighs, or a combination of thighs and bone-in skin-on breasts

2 medium carrots, sliced thin

1 cup (75 g) celery, sliced thin on the diagonal

1 red waxy potato (about 8 ounces, or 225 g), peeled and chopped fine

6 to 8 ounces (168 to 225 g) zucchini, quartered lengthwise and then sliced thin

8 cups (1.9 l) low-sodium chicken broth

3 tablespoons (48 g) tomato paste

3 bay leaves

1 tablespoon (3 g) crumbled dried Mexican oregano or marjoram

2 teaspoons (5 g) ground cumin

2 teaspoons (6 g) kosher salt or coarse sea salt, or more to taste

½ pound (225 g) fresh spinach, chopped

GARNISHES

2 cups (230 g) Monterey Jack or Chihuahua cheese

1 dozen corn tortillas, cut in thin strips and fried in oil briefly until crisp, or several large handfuls tortilla chips, broken into bite-size pieces

2 ripe avocados, diced

Chopped fresh cilantro

Lime wedges

① Generously spray the inside of the slow cooker with oil.

② Roast the tomatoes whole. Use a stovetop grill, such as an *asador*, any other grill, or place them on a baking sheet and run them under your broiler. Whatever method you choose, you want to really blacken the skins on all sides, so turn as needed. When the tomatoes are roasted, transfer them to a blender and add the onion, garlic, chipotle chiles, and adobo sauce.

③ Arrange the chicken pieces in the bottom of the slow cooker, then cover with the blended tomato mixture, carrots, celery, potato, zucchini, broth, tomato paste, bay leaves, oregano, cumin, and salt. Cover and cook on the low heat setting for 5 to 6 hours, until the chicken pieces are all cooked through and the stock is very flavorful. Discard the bay leaves. With tongs or a slotted spoon, remove the chicken pieces. When cool enough to handle, discard the skin and bones and shred the chicken into bite-size pieces.

4. Return the chicken to the soup stock and add the spinach. Cover and cook about 15 more minutes, long enough for the chicken to heat back through and the spinach to wilt. Season as needed with additional salt and pepper.

5. Divide the cheese between the bowls. Ladle the soup into the bowls, being sure to get some of all of the vegetables into each portion. Then top each with an equal portion of tortillas, avocado, and cilantro. Serve the bowls with a lime wedge to squeeze over the soup.

TORTILLA SOUP HAS ITS ORIGINS IN MEXICO AS A WAY TO USE UP OLD TORTILLAS AND LEFTOVER CHICKEN, BUT THERE, AND IN TEXAS, IT HAS COME QUITE A LONG WAY SINCE THEN.

PIGS IN A BATH

YIELD: SERVES 8 OR MORE | COOKING TIME: APPROXIMATELY 2 HOURS ON LOW, OR 1 ON HIGH, CAN BE HELD ON WARM UP TO 3 HOURS

Cocktail sausages are just plain cute. Kids love them, as does anyone who still has a smidgen of childlike delight in them. Sure, you can throw together the classic online recipe of grape jelly with barbecue sauce and call it a dish. This isn't much harder and gets you something more party worthy. These can be held on the warm setting throughout a party without loss of quality. If they sauce gets overly thick, stir in a bit of water to thin it. Another "bath" you can use for a cocktail sausage variation is Jezebel sauce, page 96.

Vegetable oil spray

1 can (8 ounces, or 225 g) crushed pineapple

1 bottle (12 ounces, or 355 ml) chili sauce (the ketchup-like condiment)

2 tablespoons (30 g) Dijon mustard

2 fresh jalapeño chiles, seeds removed, sliced in thin rounds

2 pounds (905 g) cocktail sausages, such as Lit'l Smokies

① Generously spray the inside of the slow cooker with oil.

② Combine in the slow cooker the pineapple, chili sauce, mustard, and jalapeños. Stir in the cocktail sausages. Cover and cook on the low setting for 2 hours or on high for 1 hour.

③ For a casual gathering, serve these in the slow cooker on the warming setting, with bamboo skewers or fondue forks for spearing the sausages. Leftovers keep well for up to a few days.

BLACK BEAN SOUP WITH PICO DE GALLO

YIELD: SERVES 6 OR MORE | COOKING TIME: 9 TO 11 HOURS ON LOW, 5 TO 6 HOURS ON HIGH, CAN BE HELD ON WARM FOR 2 MORE HOURS

Use a store-bought pico de gallo, or any recipe for the chunky Lone Star favorite, a blend of chopped tomatoes, onions, jalapeño or serrano chile, cilantro, and some lime juice.

2 tablespoons (30 ml) vegetable oil or olive oil (divided)

2 medium onions, chopped fine

6 plump garlic cloves, minced

1 pound (455 g) dry black beans, picked over and rinsed

1 large carrot, grated

3 bay leaves

2 teaspoons (10 g) brown sugar

1 teaspoon white vinegar or cider vinegar

½ teaspoon Maggi sauce or soy sauce

3 cups (705 ml) low-sodium chicken broth

3 cups (705 ml) water

2 tablespoons (30 ml) mezcal (preferred) or tequila, optional

1 teaspoon kosher salt or coarse sea salt

Pico de gallo

① Generously grease the inside of the slow cooker with about 1 teaspoon of the oil.

② Warm the rest of the oil in a medium skillet over medium heat. Add the onions and sauté until limp and translucent, about 5 minutes. Stir in the garlic and continue cooking about 3 minutes more, until the onions are tender.

③ Pour the black beans into the slow cooker. Spoon the onion mixture over the beans. Add the carrot, bay leaves, brown sugar, vinegar, and Maggi sauce, then pour in the broth and water. Cover and cook until beans are quite tender, 9 to 11 hours on the low heat setting, or 5 to 6 hours on high. Discard the bay leaves.

④ Remove about 1 cup of the beans and mash them with a large fork or potato masher. Return the beans to the pan, Add the mezcal, if you wish. Stir together and heat for about 15 more minutes.

⑤ Ladle into bowls. Top with pico de gallo, and serve.

TEX-CZECH BEEF, POTATO, AND BARLEY SOUP

YIELD: SERVES 6 OR MORE | COOKING TIME: 10 TO 11 HOURS ON LOW, 5 TO 6 HOURS ON HIGH, CAN BE HELD ON WARM FOR 1 MORE HOUR

This hearty mix is inspired by the central European cooking traditions that are still alive in the heart of Texas. It's just the thing for a cool evening.

Vegetable oil spray

2 tablespoons (30 ml) vegetable oil (divided)

1½ cups (240 g) diced onion (about 1 very large)

1 medium carrot, diced

4 ounces (115 g) beef chuck, diced in ½-inch (1-cm) pieces

1 tablespoon (16 g) tomato paste

4 cups (940 ml) beef broth, preferably low-sodium (divided)

6 ounces (168 g) red waxy potatoes, peeled and diced in ½-inch (1-cm) pieces

½ cup (100 g) pearled barley

1 tablespoon (3 g) dried dill

Kosher salt or coarse sea salt

1. Generously spray the inside of the slow cooker with oil.

2. Warm 1 tablespoon (15 ml) of the oil in a heavy medium skillet or saucepan over medium heat. Sauté the onion and carrot in the oil until the onion is translucent, about 5 minutes. Scrape the mixture into the slow cooker.

3. Return the skillet to the stove and raise the heat to medium-high. Add the remaining oil to the skillet. When shimmering, stir in the beef and sear on all sides to medium-brown. Stir in the tomato paste and let the mixture cook for several minutes, until the tomato paste has darkened a couple of shades and the meat sticks here and there to the bottom of the skillet. We are cooking up layers of flavor here. Stir in 1 cup (235 ml) of the broth and scrape the mixture up from the bottom, loosening all the brown bits. Scrape this mixture into the slow cooker.

4. Add to the slow cooker the remaining broth, the barley, dill, and salt to taste. Cook the soup on low for 10 to 11 hours or on the high heat setting for 5 to 6 hours. The beef, potatoes, and barley will be very soft and the soup will be fairly creamy from its long cooking time.

5. Serve hot, ladled into bowls.

BLUE CRAB AND CORN SOUP

YIELD: SERVES 6 OR MORE | COOKING TIME: 3½ TO 4¼ HOURS ON LOW

I think very few things are better together than summer corn and blue crab from the Gulf of Mexico. Together they make a superlative, lightly creamy soup. Low-fat buttermilk lends a lot of the creaminess to the soup and a little tang that's quite fitting, too.

2 tablespoons (28 g) unsalted butter (divided)

1 large onion, chopped fine

4 garlic cloves, minced

1 teaspoon tomato paste

2 tablespoons (16 g) unbleached all-purpose flour

2 cups (470 ml) low-sodium chicken, seafood, or vegetable broth

12 ounces (340 g) red-skinned potatoes, diced fine

1 cup (164 g) corn kernels

½ red bell pepper, diced fine

1 teaspoon kosher salt or other coarse salt, or more to taste

1 cup (235 ml) buttermilk

¼ cup (60 ml) half-and-half

1 pound (455 g) blue crabmeat

Fresh thyme sprigs or chives for garnish, optional

① Generously grease the inside of the slow cooker with about 1 teaspoon of the butter.

② Warm the remaining butter in a medium skillet over medium heat. Add the onion and sauté until limp and translucent, about 5 minutes. Add the garlic and continue cooking until the onion is tender, about 3 more minutes. Stir in the tomato paste, followed by the flour. Cook for 1 minute. Stir in the broth, scraping up any browned bits from the bottom. Transfer to the slow cooker.

③ Add to the slow cooker the potatoes, corn, bell pepper, and salt. Cover and cook for 3 to 3½ hours. Stir in the buttermilk, half-and-half, crabmeat, and more salt, if needed. Continue cooking covered for 30 to 45 minutes.

④ Ladle soup out into bowls, garnish with thyme sprigs, if you wish, and serve.

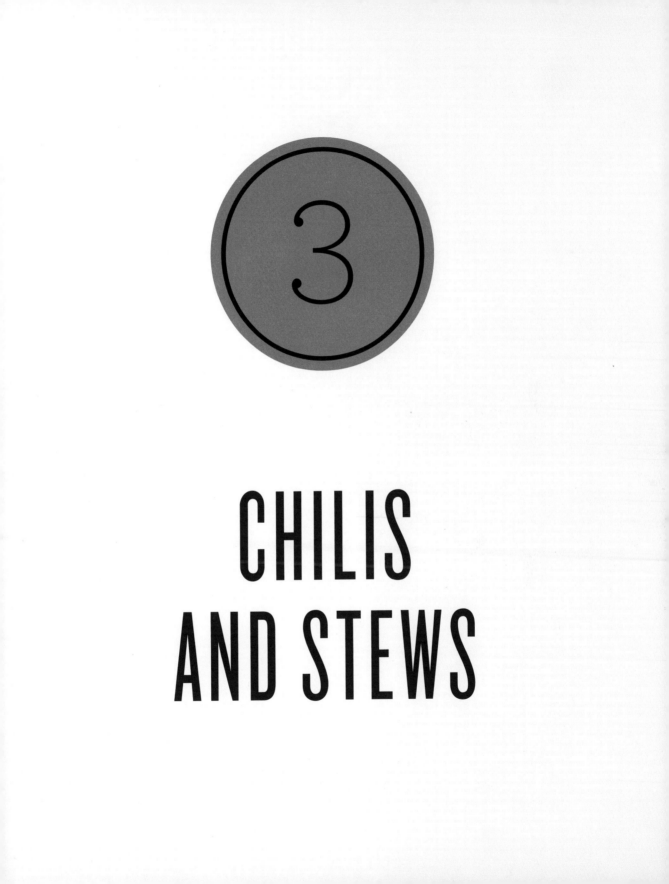

CHILIS
AND STEWS

★ CHILI AND STEWS ★

A CLASSIC BOWL OF TEXAS RED

YIELD: SERVES 8 | COOKING TIME: 6½ TO 7½ HOURS ON LOW, CAN BE HELD ON WARM FOR SEVERAL HOURS

Here's our family's classic Texas chili con carne, a meat dish, not a soup, and never, never including beans. It's the style Dallas journalist Frank X. Tolbert codified in his cult classic, *A Bowl of Red* (1953). Never has enthusiasm for the dish waned. In fact, since the advent of the slow cooker, it and other chili preparations may have become even more popular. Find mole paste in the Mexican section of a well-stocked supermarket, or at a Mexican market, or from melissaguerra.com.

Vegetable oil spray

4 bacon slices, chopped

4-pound (1.8-kg) chuck roast, trimmed of surface fat and cut in ½-inch (1-cm) cubes

1 large onion, chopped

4 plump garlic cloves, minced

½ cup (60 g) chili powder

1 tablespoon (7 g) ground cumin

1 tablespoon (16 g) black mole paste

2 teaspoons (2 g) crumbled dried oregano

2 teaspoons (6 g) kosher salt or coarse sea salt, or more to taste

2 teaspoons (10 ml) cider vinegar

2 cups (470 ml) low-sodium beef broth

Ground cayenne pepper, optional

1 to 2 tablespoons (9 to 18 g) masa harina

Chopped onions, minced fresh or pickled jalapeños, and saltine crackers for accompaniments, optional

① Generously spray the inside of the slow cooker with oil.

② Fry the bacon in a large heavy skillet over medium heat until brown and crisp. Remove the bacon from the drippings with a slotted spoon and reserve it. Stir in the beef, and sauté it until it loses its raw color. Add the onion and continue to sauté until limp. Mix in the garlic and sauté until the onion is translucent and tender. Scrape the mixture into the slow cooker.

③ Add the reserved bacon, the chili powder, cumin, mole paste, oregano, salt, and vinegar. Pour in just enough broth to cover. Cook on the low heat setting for 6 to 7 hours. When the beef is tender, taste and add a pinch, or several, of cayenne if you wish to bump up the heat level. Stir in the masa harina to thicken or "tighten" the chili, and cook on low for about 30 minutes more.

④ Serve the chili immediately, or cool, refrigerate overnight, and reheat. Serve steaming hot in bowls, with garnishes as you wish.

× CHILI AND RICE ×

Shanghai Jimmy was a Dallas character with a hole-in-the-wall joint where he customized chili eleven ways. The basic number one was a bowl of rice topped with chili. The other numbers allowed further embellishments including cheese, salsa, chopped onions and celery, oyster crackers, and sweet pickle relish. Feel free to embellish as you wish, but just steamy white or brown rice topped with chili is nice to me.

CHILI WITH TOMATOES

YIELD: SERVES 6 TO 8 | COOKING TIME: 6 TO 7 HOURS, CAN BE HELD ON WARM FOR SEVERAL HOURS

Some folks argue about whether classic Texas chili should have tomatoes. I figure if my friend Tom Perini, iconic Texas cook, owner of the much-lauded Perini Ranch Steakhouse outside of Abilene, puts tomatoes in chili, then I should have a recipe that includes them too. I could eat three or four bowls of this just while arguing the point.

Vegetable oil spray

2 pounds (905 g) chili-grind (coarsely ground) beef

1 medium onion, chopped

2 garlic cloves, minced

1 teaspoon crumbled dried Mexican oregano or marjoram

¾ teaspoon ground cumin

2 tablespoons (15 g) chili powder

1½ teaspoons kosher salt or coarse sea salt, or more to taste

1 or 2 fresh jalapeño chiles, minced

1 tablespoon (15 ml) vegetable oil

2 medium red bell peppers, chopped

1 green bell pepper, chopped

1 can (15 ounces, or 425 g) diced tomatoes with juice

1 cup (235 ml) low-sodium beef broth

① Generously spray the inside of the slow cooker with oil.

② Sauté the beef in a large heavy skillet over medium heat until it loses its raw color. Add the onion and sauté briefly until softened. Mix in the garlic, oregano, cumin, chili powder, salt, and jalapeños, and sauté another minute or 2, until the mixture is fragrant. Scrape the mixture into the slow cooker. Return the skillet to the cooktop. Pour in the oil and warm it over medium heat. Stir in the bell peppers and cook 7 to 10 minutes, until tender. Scrape the bell pepper mixture into the slow cooker.

③ Pour the tomatoes and broth into the slow cooker. Cover it. Cook the chili on the low heat setting for 6 to 7 hours, until the beef is extremely tender and the vegetables have melded together.

④ Serve the chili immediately, or cool, refrigerate overnight, and reheat. Serve steaming hot in bowls.

CHICKEN CHORIZO CHILI

YIELD: SERVES 8 | COOKING TIME: 5 TO 6 HOURS ON LOW, CAN BE HELD UP TO 2 HOURS ON WARM

Among the national debuts of chili was inclusion in the second, 1906 edition of Fannie Farmer's landmark *Boston Cooking-School Cook Book.* She made it with "two young chickens" and "red peppers" or "canned pimientos." That gives you a sense of how much the average Bostonian of the early twentieth century knew about *real* chili. It is possible though to stretch the idea of chicken chili to a satisfying conclusion. I have used hominy as a bulk ingredient here. Feel free to use a similar amount of canned white beans, if it fits your mood or pantry's condition.

Vegetable oil spray

1 pound (455 g) bulk Mexican-style chorizo

1 large yellow onion, chopped

2 medium celery stalks, chopped fine

1 tablespoon (8 g) chili powder

1 teaspoon ground cumin

1 teaspoon kosher salt or coarse sea salt

2 pounds (905 g) boneless skinless chicken thighs, in ½-inch (1-cm) cubes

1 jar (8 ounces, or 225 g) roasted piquillo peppers or other red peppers, chopped fine

1 can (15 ounces, or 425 g) white or yellow hominy, drained and rinsed

1½ cups (355 ml) low-sodium chicken broth

Shredded Monterey Jack cheese or fresh cilantro leaves for garnish, optional,

① Generously spray the inside of the slow cooker with oil.

② Fry the chorizo in a medium skillet over medium-high heat. Break up large clumps of the chorizo with a spatula or wooden spoon while it cooks. When the chorizo has lost its raw color, add to it the onion and celery, and continue cooking for 5 to 8 more minutes until the vegetables are tender. Sprinkle in the chili powder, cumin, and salt, and cook for another couple of minutes to blend the flavor of the spices.

③ Scrape the mixture into the slow cooker. Add the uncooked chicken, peppers, hominy, and broth. Cover and cook on the low heat setting for 5 to 6 hours. The hominy should have broken down somewhat and thickened the liquid.

④ Serve hot, spooned into bowls. Garnish, if you wish, with sprinklings of cheese and cilantro leaves.

VENISON CHILI

YIELD: SERVES 6 OR MORE | COOKING TIME: 5 TO 6 HOURS ON LOW, CAN BE HELD ON WARM FOR UP TO 2 HOURS

Some years ago, long before my career involved writing about food, I attended a cooking class taught by Dallas chef Stephan Pyles. In it, he demonstrated a tamale tart, his fanciful chef's re-creation of the homey tamale pie. It featured a masa harina shell, roasted garlic custard, and a topping of venison chili. Much as I liked the dish, and Stephan, I never have gotten around to making the tart. What I do make however, is a simplified version of his chili. I have changed up the cooking style just a bit to make the dish more slow-cooker friendly. Remember that venison is a good bit leaner than beef so you need to cook it with a bit more fat to give it that full mouthfeel a great chili needs. I top it off with goat cheese from Paula Lambert's Mozzarella Company. Also a Dallas culinary star, Paula was among the first people to take my interest in food writing seriously and open doors for me.

¼ cup (59 ml) vegetable oil (divided)

¼ cup (59 ml) bacon drippings or additional vegetable oil

1 large onion, chopped

8 plump garlic cloves, minced

3 tablespoons (23 g) ground dried ancho chile

2 teaspoons (5 g) ground dried chipotle chile

¾ teaspoon ground cumin

1 teaspoon kosher salt or coarse sea salt, or more to taste

4 red-ripe Italian plum tomatoes, chopped

3 pounds (1.4 kg) venison leg or stew meat, finely chopped

1 cup (235 ml) low-sodium beef broth

1 cup (235 ml) low-sodium chicken broth

6 to 8 ounces (168 to 225 g) crumbled creamy fresh goat cheese, such as Mozzarella Company, for garnish

① Grease the inside of the slow cooker with about 1 teaspoon of the oil.

② Warm the remaining oil and bacon drippings in a large heavy skillet over medium heat. Stir in the onion and continue to sauté until limp. Mix in the garlic and sauté until tender, 5 to 8 more minutes. Add the ancho and chipotle chiles, cumin, 1 teaspoon salt, and sauté an additional couple of minutes to meld the flavors. Scrape the mixture into the slow cooker.

③ Add to the slow cooker the tomatoes, venison, and both broths. Stir together. Cover and cook on the low heat setting for 5 to 6 hours until the meat is very tender and the vegetables reduced to a sauce. Add more salt, if you wish.

④ Serve the chili immediately, or cool, refrigerate overnight, and reheat. Serve hot in bowls, with goat cheese crumbled over each portion.

TURKEY–BLACK BEAN CHILI

YIELD: SERVES 8 | COOKING TIME: 5 TO 6 HOURS ON LOW, CAN BE HELD ON WARM FOR 2 HOURS

If I'm not opting for a beefy chili, this is my personal fallback favorite. Perhaps it's a little healthier by current medical thought, but it's also super tasty.

2 tablespoons (30 ml) vegetable oil (divided)

1 large onion, chopped (about 1 cup [160 g])

1 green bell pepper, chopped

4 plump garlic cloves, minced

1½ pounds (680 g) chili-grind (coarsely ground) turkey thighs or other dark meat

2 tablespoons (15 g) chili powder

2 teaspoons (5 g) ground dried chipotle chile, or more to taste

2 teaspoons (5 g) ground cumin

2 teaspoons (6 g) kosher salt or coarse sea salt

1 bay leaf

3 cans (15 ounces, or 425 g each) black beans, drained and rinsed

1 can (8 ounces, or 225 g) tomato sauce

Approximately 3 cups (705 ml) low-sodium chicken broth

Sour cream for garnish, optional

① Generously grease the inside of the slow cooker with 1 teaspoon of the oil.

② Warm the remaining oil in a large heavy skillet over medium heat. Stir in the onion and sauté until limp, about 3 minutes. Mix in the bell pepper and garlic. Sauté until tender, 5 to 8 more minutes. Add in the turkey, and sauté it just until it loses its raw color. Scrape the mixture into the slow cooker.

③ Add the chili powder, chipotle chile, cumin, salt, and bay leaf. Add the beans and tomato sauce, and stir together. Pour in just enough broth to cover the beans and meat mixture. Cover and cook on the low heat setting for 5 to 6 hours. Discard the bay leaf.

④ Serve the chili immediately, or cool, refrigerate overnight, and reheat. Serve hot in bowls, with sour cream, if you wish.

CHILI MAC

YIELD: SERVES 6 OR MORE | COOKING TIME: 3 TO 3½ HOURS ON HIGH

Chili mac is as much about macaroni, beans, and tomatoes, as it is about the beef itself.

Vegetable oil spray

¾ pound (340 g) lean ground beef

1 medium onion, minced

8 ounces (½ pound, or 225 g) uncooked elbow macaroni

3 cups (705 ml) low-sodium beef broth, preferably, or chicken broth

1 can (15 ounces, or 425 g) chili beans, undrained

1 can (10 ounces, or 280 g) diced tomatoes and green chiles, such as Ro-Tel

2 garlic cloves, minced

1 tablespoon (8 g) chili powder

2 teaspoons (6 g) kosher salt or coarse sea salt

1½ teaspoons ground cumin

Shredded mild Cheddar cheese for garnish, optional

① Generously spray the inside of the slow cooker with oil.

② Sauté ground beef in a heavy medium or large skillet over medium-high heat, breaking it apart with a spatula while it cooks. As soon as it loses its raw color, mix in the onion and continue cooking about 5 more minutes, until the beef is just cooked through and the onion has softened.

③ Scrape the mixture from the skillet into the slow cooker. Add the remaining ingredients (except the optional cheese) and stir together, making sure the macaroni is covered with liquid.

④ Cook on high approximately 3 hours, until the macaroni is tender. The mixture should remain a bit soupy.

⑤ Serve hot in bowls. If you wish, top each bowl with 1 to 2 tablespoons (8 to 15 g) of cheese.

PORK CHILE VERDE, HOMESICK TEXAN STYLE

YIELD: SERVES 6 TO 8 | COOKING TIME: 8½ TO 9½ HOURS ON LOW, 4½ TO 5½ HOURS ON HIGH, CAN BE HELD ON WARM FOR SEVERAL HOURS

Saveur magazine called "The Homesick Texan" the country's Best Regional Food Blog. Lisa Fain is the talented and displaced Houstonian behind the blog's tall tales and scrumptious recipes. Remember the old Pace picante sauce commercial where the crusty cowboys made fun of a salsa made in New York City? Well, that's where Lisa lives, but she has her strong sensibility about classic Texas eats. With her permission, I have modified a recipe for the slow cooker from *The Homesick Texan's Family Table* (Ten Speed Press, 2014).

2 tablespoons (30 ml) bacon drippings or vegetable oil

Kosher salt or coarse sea salt

Freshly ground black pepper

4 pounds (1.8 kg) boneless pork shoulder, cut into 1-inch (2.5-cm) cubes

1 large yellow onion, diced

6 cloves garlic, chopped

1 pound (455 g) tomatillos, husked and halved

2 tablespoons (28 g) ground cumin

2 tablespoons (6 g) crumbled dried oregano

½ teaspoon ground allspice

1½ cups (355 ml) low-sodium chicken broth (divided)

12 ounces (355 ml) beer, preferably a Mexican lager, such as Bohemia

4 fresh poblano chiles, roasted, peeled, seeded, and diced

4 fresh jalapeño chiles, seeded and diced

1 cup (16 g) chopped fresh cilantro

1 tablespoon (15 ml) fresh lime juice

2 tablespoons (18 g) masa harina or cornmeal

Grated Monterey Jack cheese and sour cream, for garnish

① Generously grease the inside of the slow cooker with 1 teaspoon of the bacon drippings. Sprinkle salt and pepper over the pork cubes.

② Warm the rest of the bacon drippings in a large heavy skillet over medium heat. Stir in the onion and cook until limp, about 3 minutes. Add the garlic and the tomatillos, and cook until the onion has softened and tomatillos are crisp-tender, about 5 more minutes. Add the cumin, oregano, and allspice, and cook an additional minute until fragrant. Scrape the mixture into the slow cooker.

③ Add one-half of the pork cubes to the skillet and cook over high heat just until the meat has lost its raw color. Scrape into the slow cooker. Add the rest of the pork, and again cook over high heat just until the meat has lost its raw color. Pour in about ½ cup (120 ml) of the broth and scrape browned bits up from the bottom of the skillet. Pour the mixture, the rest of the broth, and the beer into the slow cooker. Top with the poblano and jalapeño chiles. Cover and cook for 8 to 9 hours on low, or 4 to 5 hours on high, until the pork is very tender and vegetables have cooked down. Stir in the cilantro, lime juice, and masa harina to thicken or "tighten" the chili. Cook on low for about 30 minutes more.

④ Serve in bowls with cheese and sour cream.

REMEMBER THE OLD PACE PICANTE SAUCE COMMERCIAL WHERE THE CRUSTY COWBOYS MADE FUN OF A SALSA MADE IN NEW YORK CITY? WELL, THAT'S WHERE LISA FAIN, "THE HOMESICK TEXAN," LIVES, BUT LISA HAS RETAINED HER VERY STRONG SENSIBILITY ABOUT CLASSIC TEXAS EATS.

GREEN CHILE STEW

YIELD: SERVES 6 OR MORE | COOKING TIME: 7 TO 8 HOURS ON LOW, CAN BE HELD ON WARM FOR SEVERAL HOURS

The HEB and Whole Foods grocery stores, in particular, have popularized the fall crop of freshly harvested, long, green, New Mexican chiles, often marketed as Hatch chiles. Prior to these recent marketing campaigns, New Mexican–style green chile pods weren't much known beyond the far western fringes of Texas. To set the record straight, I feel the need to explain that Hatch, New Mexico, is just one area of the state where chiles grow, rather than a variety of chile. You can make a luscious stew out of any of the state's signature pungent pods. On its home turf, green chile stew is more often made with pork, but beef is perhaps even tastier. Accompany, if you wish, with fluffy flour tortillas.

2 tablespoons (30 ml) vegetable oil

2 medium onions, chopped

5 plump garlic cloves, minced

1 tablespoon (16 g) tomato paste

1 tablespoon (8 g) unbleached
all-purpose flour

1 cup (235 ml) low-sodium beef broth

2 pounds (905 g) beef chuck,
cut in 1-inch (2.5-cm) cubes

3 cups (705 ml) chicken broth,
preferably low-sodium

2 teaspoons (10 ml) soy sauce
or ½ teaspoon Maggi sauce

½ teaspoon kosher salt or coarse salt

1½ pounds (680 g) waxy red potatoes,
cut in ½-inch (1-cm) cubes

3 cups (450 g) chopped, peeled, fresh,
or frozen, New Mexican green chiles
(divided)

1 cup (164 g) corn kernels, fresh
or frozen

① Generously spray the inside of the slow cooker with oil.

② Warm the oil in a large heavy skillet over medium heat. Stir in the onions and garlic. Cook until translucent, about 5 minutes. Mix in the tomato paste and the flour. Cook for 2 to 3 minutes more, until somewhat browned and fragrant. Pour in the beef broth and scrape the mixture up from the bottom to get all the tasty browned bits. Scrape the mixture into the slow cooker.

③ Add to the slow cooker the beef cubes, chicken broth, soy sauce, salt, potatoes, and 1 cup (150 g) of the green chiles. Cook on the low heat setting for approximately 7 to 8 hours. When the beef and potatoes are tender, stir in the remaining green chiles and corn. Continue cooking for about 30 more minutes until heated through.

④ Serve piping hot, ladled into bowls.

BEEF STEW

YIELD: SERVES 6 OR MORE | COOKING TIME: 8 TO 9 HOURS ON LOW, CAN BE HELD ON WARM FOR SEVERAL HOURS

While researching Texas foods, I came across some promotional information about a 1930s-era cattlemen's contest for favorite stew recipes. The winning cowboy called his recipe "Stew without Them Goddamn Carrots." I don't think he'd like mine, but I am hoping that you will.

Vegetable oil spray

4 thick-cut bacon slices, chopped

3 pounds (1.4 kg) boneless beef chuck, cut in 1-inch (2.5-cm) cubes

2 tablespoons (16 g) unbleached all-purpose flour

1 tablespoon (8 g) ground dried ancho chile

2 cups (470 ml) low-sodium beef broth (divided)

4 medium carrots, cut in half lengthwise and then into ½-inch-thick (1-cm) half-moons

2 medium russet (baking) potatoes, peeled and cut into ½-inch (1-cm) cubes

1½ cups (150 g) frozen pearl onions, unthawed

2 tablespoons (32 g) tomato paste

1½ teaspoons kosher salt or coarse sea salt

1 teaspoon yellow mustard

2 bay leaves

12 ounces (355 ml) beer, preferably a Mexican lager, such as Bohemia

① Generously spray the inside of the slow cooker with oil.

② In a large heavy skillet, fry the bacon over medium-low heat until brown and crisp. Remove the bacon with a slotted spoon and transfer it to the slow cooker. Turn the heat up to medium-high. In the bacon drippings, brown the meat, about one-third of it at a time. Turn on all sides as needed, then transfer to the slow cooker. When the third batch of beef is mostly browned, sprinkle in the flour and the ancho chile, and cook for a couple of additional minutes. Pour in about ½ cup (120 ml) of the broth, and scrape the mixture up from the bottom of the pan. Scrape into the slow cooker.

③ Add to the slow cooker the carrots, potatoes, pearl onions, tomato paste, salt, mustard, bay leaves, beer, and the rest of the beef broth. Stir up from the bottom. Cover and cook for 8 to 9 hours on the low heat setting, until the meat and vegetables are quite tender. Discard the bay leaves.

④ Serve up hot in big bowls.

BEEF AND TEXAS RED WINE STEW

YIELD: SERVES 8 | COOKING TIME: 8 TO 9 HOURS ON LOW, 4 TO 5 HOURS ON HIGH, CAN BE HELD ON WARM FOR SEVERAL HOURS

Though inspired by beef bourguignon, this stew resides firmly in the heart of Texas. It takes on the character of the wine used in it. Select a red with style but moderate price, such as a Texas cabernet from Kiepersol Estate or the Rhone-style blended red table wine from McPherson Cellars called Les Copains. This is a bit involved, but makes enough to serve a party over noodles or spaetzle. Leftovers are fabulous.

Vegetable oil spray

6 ounces (168 g) thick-sliced bacon, chopped

3 pounds (1.4 kg) boneless beef chuck, cut in 2-inch (5-cm) cubes

3 tablespoons (24 g) unbleached all-purpose flour

3 cups (705 ml) dry red wine (divided)

2 cups (470 ml) low-sodium beef broth

3 cups (480 g) chopped onions

6 medium carrots, cut in 2-inch (5-cm) lengths

3 plump garlic cloves, minced

1 tablespoon (16 g) tomato paste

1 teaspoon dried thyme

2 bay leaves

2 teaspoons (6 g) kosher salt or coarse sea salt, or more to taste

2 tablespoons (28 g) unsalted butter

¾ pound (340 g) cremini mushrooms or button mushrooms, sliced thickly

2 cups (200 g) frozen pearl onions, unthawed

½ cup (30 g) chopped Italian flat-leaf parsley

① Generously spray the inside of the slow cooker with oil.

② In a large heavy skillet, fry the bacon over medium-low heat until brown and crisp. Remove the bacon with a slotted spoon and transfer it to the slow cooker. Turn the heat up to medium-high. In the bacon drippings, brown the meat, about one-third of it at a time. Turn on all sides as needed, then transfer to the slow cooker. When the third batch of beef is mostly browned, sprinkle in the flour, and cook for a couple of additional minutes. Pour in about ½ cup (120 ml) of the wine, and scrape the mixture up from the bottom of the pan. Scrape into the slow cooker.

③ Add 2 more cups (470 ml) of the wine, the broth, onions, carrots, garlic, tomato paste, thyme, bay leaves, and salt. Cover and cook on the low heat setting for 8 to 9 hours, or for 4 to 5 hours on high. The beef should be very tender and the onions and carrots mostly dissolved into the sauce.

④ In large heavy skillet, warm the butter over medium heat. Stir in the mushrooms and cook for several minutes until limp. Add the pearl onions and cover the skillet for 5 minutes. Uncover and pour in the remaining ½ cup of wine. Cook several minutes more, until the onions are tender and the wine has reduced somewhat. Transfer to the slow cooker and stir well.

⑤ Discard the bay leaves. Add more salt, if you wish. Spoon into shallow bowls, scatter each with parsley, and serve.

SOUTH TEXAS VENISON STEW

YIELD: SERVES 6 | COOKING TIME: 8 TO 9 HOURS ON LOW, CAN BE HELD ON WARM FOR AN ADDITIONAL HOUR

I've created versions of this stew over more than three decades. I think some of the inspiration must have come from a visit with Mike Hughes, the founder of Broken Arrow Ranch, near Kerrville. Mike's son, Chris, manages the ranch and the venison today. The herds are non-native species like axis deer and Nilgai antelope. The meat is never gamey because of its high-quality immediate processing. The common white-tail deer, hunted around the state in season, cannot be sold commercially because, technically, it belongs to the state of Texas. You might manage though to score some from a hunter friend. Whatever the kind of venison, you want a braising cut for this dish, what would be cut up as stew meat. You can order Broken Arrow Ranch venison from brokenarrowranch.com, though many Texas supermarkets carry farmed venison.

Vegetable oil spray

1 large onion, diced

1 large red bell pepper, diced

4 plump garlic cloves, minced

¾ cup (96 g) diced dried apricots

2 cups (470 ml) low-sodium beef broth

¼ cup plus 2 tablespoons (90 g) chili sauce (the ketchup-style condiment)

1½ teaspoons kosher salt or coarse sea salt

1 teaspoon coarse-ground black pepper

1 teaspoon ground cumin

2 pounds (905 g) venison stew meat, in ¾-inch (2-cm) cubes

1 can (15 ounces, or 425 g) hominy, drained

1 can (15 ounces, or 425 g) black beans, drained and rinsed

Juice of 1 large lime

Cilantro leaves, for garnish

① Generously spray the inside of the slow cooker with oil.

② Combine in the slow cooker the onion, bell pepper, garlic, and apricots. Pour in the broth and chili sauce.

③ Combine the salt, pepper, and cumin, and toss with the venison cubes. Rub the seasonings in with your fingers. Transfer the venison to the slow cooker. Cover and cook for 8 to 9 hours on the low heat setting. When the venison is quite tender, stir in the hominy, beans, and lime juice. Cover and cook for about 30 more minutes, until heated through.

④ Ladle the stew into bowls, top each with a small handful of cilantro leaves, and serve.

HOPKINS COUNTY CHICKEN STEW

YIELD: SERVES 6 TO 8 | COOKING TIME: 7 TO 8 HOURS ON LOW, 3½ TO 4 HOURS ON HIGH, CAN BE HELD ON WARM FOR AN ADDITIONAL HOUR

Sulphur Springs is home to the World Champion Hopkins County Stew Contest. Held each October, teams cook up their recipes in iron cauldrons over wood fires while wearing turn-of-the-last-century period dress. Oh my, there's surely nothing like stirring fifty gallons of stew over flames for hours while wearing a lovely gingham dress and bonnet. It's a lot simpler to take liberties with the cooking method and turn it into a slow-cooker dish. Get a bit of the smokiness that comes from cooking in the outdoors over live fire by using smoked salt and smoked paprika. Using thighs will give you the moistest chicken, but lots of people will just prefer white meat. Your call, or mix them up.

1 tablespoon (14 g) unsalted butter (divided)

3 medium baking potatoes, peeled and diced

1 large onion, diced

2 pounds (905 g) skin-on bone-in chicken thighs, breasts, or a combination

4 cups (940 ml) low-sodium chicken broth

1 can (15 ounces, or 425 g) crushed tomatoes

1 can (15 ounces, or 425 g) tomato sauce

1 teaspoon Maggi sauce or soy sauce

2 teaspoons (5 g) chili powder

2 teaspoons (5 g) smoked paprika

2 teaspoons (10 g) smoked salt, such as Maldon

1 teaspoon coarse-ground black pepper

2 cups (328 g) corn kernels, fresh or frozen

1 can (15½ ounces, or 440 g) creamed corn

Grated Cheddar cheese, for garnish

1. Generously grease the inside of the slow cooker with about 1 teaspoon of the butter.

2. Combine in the slow cooker the potatoes, onion, chicken, and broth. Cover and cook on the low heat setting for 5 to 6 hours or on high for 3 hours. Remove the chicken pieces with tongs or a slotted spoon. When the chicken is cool enough to handle, discard skin and bones. Dice the chicken and return it to the pot. Add the remaining ingredients, including the rest of the butter, and cook for at least 2 more hours on low or about 1 more hour on high. The stew should be fairly thick and cooked down.

3. Ladle into bowls and garnish with Cheddar cheese. Serve piping hot.

HILL COUNTRY GOULASH

YIELD: SERVES 6 | COOKING TIME: 6 TO 7 HOURS ON LOW, 3 TO 4 HOURS ON HIGH, CAN BE HELD FOR SEVERAL HOURS ON WARM

When I talked to my stepdaughter, a longtime Austin and Hill Country resident, about what absolutely *had* to be in this book, one of her first answers was goulash. The dish came before a lot of more "Texan" things, to my mind, but I made note of its importance to her. I must credit fellow food writer Robb Walsh for making the full connection—for me and others—between goulash and chili in his *Texas Eats: The New Lone Star Heritage Cookbook*. German-born William Gebhardt, the creator of the classic Gebhardt's Eagle Brand Chili Powder, was inspired to use local ancho chiles in a blend of seasonings. What he created was otherwise similar to what was used by German and Eastern European cooks to flavor goulash in the Mother Country.

Vegetable oil spray

2 tablespoons (30 ml) bacon drippings
   or vegetable oil

1½ pounds (680 g) ground chuck
   or other ground beef

1½ cups (240 g) chopped mild onion

3 garlic cloves, minced

3 tablespoons (21 g) sweet Hungarian
   paprika, or a combination of
   2 tablespoons (14 g) mild with
   1 tablespoon (7 g) hot

1½ teaspoons kosher salt or coarse
   sea salt

1 can (15 ounces, or 425 g)
   tomato sauce

1 teaspoon white vinegar
   or cider vinegar

12 ounces (340 g) elbow macaroni

Sour cream, for garnish

1. Generously spray the inside of the slow cooker with oil.

2. Sauté the beef in the bacon drippings in a large heavy skillet over medium heat until it loses its raw color. Add the onion to the drippings and sauté briefly until softened. Mix in the garlic, paprika, and salt, and sauté until the mixture is fragrant. Scrape the mixture into the slow cooker.

3. Add the tomato sauce and vinegar, and cover. Cook the goulash on the low heat setting for 6 to 7 hours, or on high for 3 to 4 hours.

4. Shortly before you are ready to serve the goulash, cook the macaroni according to the package directions. Spoon it up on plates, then ladle the goulash over it. Top each portion with a dollop of sour cream and serve.

BEEF, BISON, AND VENISON

COWTOWN BEEF POT ROAST

YIELD: SERVES 6 TO 8 | COOKING TIME: 5 TO 6 HOURS ON HIGH, 9 TO 10 HOURS ON LOW, CAN BE HELD ON WARM FOR SEVERAL HOURS

Holy cow.

Vegetable oil spray

1 tablespoon (8 g) cornstarch

½ cup (120 ml) low-sodium beef broth or chicken broth

1 can (10 ounces, or 280 g) tomatoes and green chiles, such as Ro-Tel

2 tablespoons (30 g) Worcestershire sauce

¾ pound (340 g) small Yukon gold or red waxy potatoes, halved or quartered to "2-bite" size

3 medium carrots, cut in 2-inch (5-cm) lengths

1 large onion, cut through the ends into 8 wedges

4 plump garlic cloves, halved

1 tablespoon (7 g) smoked paprika

2 teaspoons (5 g) onion powder

2 teaspoons (6 g) kosher salt or coarse sea salt

1 teaspoon freshly ground black pepper

3-pound (1.4-kg) boneless beef chuck roast

① Generously spray the inside of the slow cooker with oil.

② In the slow cooker, combine the cornstarch with 2 tablespoons (28 ml) of broth. When smooth, pour in the rest of the broth, the tomatoes and green chiles with all liquid, and the Worcestershire sauce. Add the potatoes, carrots, onion, and garlic.

③ In a small bowl, combine the paprika, onion powder, salt, and pepper, then rub the mixture all over the roast, pushing it into openings in the roast's surface. Transfer to the slow cooker.

④ Cover and cook on the high heat setting for 5 to 6 hours, or 9 to 10 hours on low until the roast and vegetables are quite tender, though short of falling apart. Let sit uncovered for about 15 minutes. Drain off the pan juices into a small saucepan and reduce to gravy thickness. Slice the roast across the grain. Serve with equal portions of vegetables, drizzled with pan juices.

VENISON POT ROAST

YIELD: SERVES 6 TO 8 | **COOKING TIME:** 4½ TO 5 HOURS ON HIGH, 9 TO 10 HOURS ON LOW

Deer, antelope, or elk meat, with its hint of gaminess, pairs well with a slightly sweet-sour flavoring here. By the way, venison should have only a slightly deeper taste than domesticated meat like beef, or else it wasn't properly processed. Because the meat is so lean, the slow cooker is one of the best ways to cook less tender cuts like a chuck roast.

Vegetable oil spray

1 tablespoon (8 g) cornstarch

½ cup (120 ml) cider vinegar

1 can (14½ ounces, or 411 g) diced tomatoes with juice

2 tablespoons (30 g) Worcestershire sauce

2 tablespoons (30 g) packed brown sugar

1 tablespoon (15 g) brown mustard

1½ teaspoons kosher salt or coarse sea salt

1 teaspoon freshly ground black pepper

1 teaspoon sweet paprika

3-pound (1.4-kg) venison chuck roast

1 large onion, sliced

2 garlic cloves, minced

① Generously spray the inside of the slow cooker with oil.

② In the slow cooker, combine the cornstarch with 2 tablespoons (28 ml) of vinegar. When smooth, pour in the rest of the vinegar, the tomatoes, Worcestershire sauce, brown sugar, and mustard.

③ In a small bowl, combine the salt, pepper, and paprika, and then rub the mixture all over the roast, pushing it into openings in the roast's surface. Transfer to the slow cooker, then top with onion and garlic.

④ Cover and cook on high for 4½ to 5 hours or on the low heat setting for 9 to 10 hours until the roast is quite tender, just short of falling apart. Let sit uncovered for about 10 minutes. Serve sliced across the grain with equal portions of pan juices.

TOM PERINI, OF THE PERINI RANCH STEAKHOUSE OUTSIDE OF ABILENE, CREATED THIS AS A BISON DISH FOR AN ANNUAL FALL EVENT CALLED COMANCHE MOON SOCIAL. YOU CAN MAKE IT WITH BEEF INSTEAD OF BISON, IF YOU LIKE, AS TOM OFTEN DOES.

BEEF OR BISON SHORT RIBS, TOM PERINI STYLE

YIELD: SERVES 4 OR MORE | COOKING TIME: 9 TO 10 HOURS ON LOW, 5 TO 6 HOURS ON HIGH

I have been known to drive miles out of my way to make a stop at the Perini Ranch Steakhouse in Buffalo Gap, a delightful village on the outskirts of Abilene. Buffalo Gap takes its name from a pass in the surrounding hills and mesas that allowed bison herds to thunder through and drink from nearby Elm Creek. More than twenty years ago, local Tom Perini decided to turn his family's ranch outside of the village into a steakhouse, thinking that cattle were more valuable to him on the plate than on the range. Tom created this as a bison dish for an annual fall event called Comanche Moon Social, but makes it more frequently with beef, since it's more economical. Tom's wife, Lisa, asked me to note that the short ribs are especially scrumptious with creamy mashed potatoes and crusty bread. Reduce the cooking time for smaller bison short ribs by an hour at either low or high.

Vegetable oil spray

3½ to 4 pounds (1.6 to 1.8 kg) meaty bone-in beef or bison short ribs

2 medium tomatoes, halved through their equators

2 fresh jalapeños, halved lengthwise

1 large onion, quartered

2 ounces (55 g) button mushrooms, halved

3 scallions, white and green portions, chopped

½ teaspoon black peppercorns

1 bay leaf

1 tablespoon (8 g) onion powder

1 teaspoon white pepper

½ teaspoon granulated garlic

½ teaspoon crumbled dried oregano

1½ teaspoons kosher salt or coarse sea salt, or more to taste

3 cups (705 ml) low-sodium beef broth

⅓ cup (80 g) Worcestershire sauce

1½ cups (355 ml) dry red wine, such as cabernet sauvignon or merlot (divided)

¼ cup (32 g) cornstarch

1. Generously spray the inside of the slow cooker with oil.

2. Toss the meat and vegetables into the slow cooker. Add the dry seasonings, then pour in the broth, Worcestershire sauce, and 1 cup (235 ml) of the wine. Cover and cook for 9 to 10 hours on the low heat setting, or 5 to 6 hours on high.

3. Remove the ribs with tongs or a slotted spoon and set them on a platter and cover with foil. Pour the vegetables and cooking liquid through a large fine strainer into a large saucepan. Push down on the vegetables to get all the juices from them. Bring the liquid to a boil over medium-high heat, and reduce the sauce by about one-third. Stir together the remaining ½ cup wine and cornstarch, and add it to the sauce. Continue cooking until the sauce thickens and has no taste of raw cornstarch, 2 to 3 more minutes.

4. Remove the bay leaf. Remove the bones from the short ribs and stir the meat back into the sauce. Heat through and serve.

FAUX Q

YIELD: SERVES 6 TO 8 | COOKING TIME: 9 TO 10 HOURS ON LOW, 5 TO 6 HOURS ON HIGH

I love the process and camaraderie of barbecuing a brisket in my Houston-made Pitts & Spitts pit. However, I often can't find the time to organize the fourteen-or-so hours I need to do it to perfection with a full packer-trimmed brisket. Neither can I drop into Austin as often as I would like to stand in barbecue genius Aaron Franklin's nearly perpetual line. So, while knowing that no slow-cooker version is going to compare to a genuine, low smoldering, wood fire, this makes a pretty darned tasty meat. I will look the other way if you want to serve it with a favorite barbecue sauce, but it's as unnecessary as on real Q. You know, as unneeded as a third horn on a longhorn.

Vegetable oil spray

2 tablespoons (34 g) smoked salt

2 tablespoons (14 g) smoked mild Spanish paprika

2 tablespoons (30 g) packed brown sugar

2 tablespoons (15 g) chili powder

2 tablespoons (12 g) freshly ground black pepper

2 tablespoons (30 g) adobo sauce from a can of chipotles in adobo sauce

2 teaspoons (10 ml) pure liquid smoke, optional

4-pound (1.8-kg) trimmed flat-cut brisket section (Don't remove any surface fat.)

① Generously spray the inside of the slow cooker with oil.

② In a small bowl, combine the salt, paprika, brown sugar, chili powder, pepper, adobo sauce, and optional liquid smoke. Rub the seasoning paste all over the brisket.

③ Transfer the brisket to the slow cooker, fat-side up. Cover and cook for 9 to 10 hours on the low heat setting, or 5 to 6 hours on high, until the meat is very tender but short of total fall-apart texture. It will have given off a good bit of liquid and fat.

④ Transfer the brisket to a cutting board. Let it sit for 10 minutes. Slice off fat for those that wish, but it's pretty amazing tasting for an occasional indulgence. Slice thinly across the grain. Eat as is, or use in sandwiches or tacos.

DR PEPPER BRAISED BRISKET

YIELD: SERVES 6 TO 8 | COOKING TIME: 9 TO 10 HOURS ON LOW, 5 TO 6 HOURS ON HIGH

Even when you're not trying to make brisket taste like it might have been barbecued, the big slab of meat reigns as one of the most sublime main dishes ever. Here's a more classic ranch-style braise. I do like a little barbecue sauce in this one, especially when it's also a Texas classic like Stubb's Smokey Mesquite. One of the cool things about Stubb's sauce is that is contains only cane sugar—no high-fructose corn syrup.

Vegetable oil spray

4-pound (1.8-kg) trimmed flat-cut brisket section

1 pound (455 g) onions, ½-inch (1-cm) slices, with rings pulled apart

½ cup (130 g) tomato-based barbecue sauce, such as Stubb's

3 tablespoons (108 g) instant tapioca

1 tablespoon (8 g) onion powder

1 tablespoon (15 g) Worcestershire sauce

1 tablespoon (15 g) kosher salt or coarse sea salt

1 bottle or can (12 ounces, or 355 ml) Dr Pepper

① Generously spray the inside of the slow cooker with oil.

② Transfer the brisket to the slow cooker, fat-side up. Scatter the onions over the brisket. Add the remaining ingredients. Cover and cook for 9 to 10 hours on the low heat setting, or 5 to 6 hours on high, until the meat is very tender but short of fall-apart texture.

③ Transfer the brisket to a cutting board. Let sit for 10 minutes, then slice thinly across the grain. Serve with some of the onion slices, and drizzle each portion with a spoonful or two of the pan juices.

FAJITAS

YIELD: SERVES 6 OR MORE | COOKING TIME: 7 TO 8 HOURS ON LOW, 4 TO 4½ HOURS ON HIGH, CAN BE HELD ON WARM FOR 1 HOUR

Who knew that the national dish of Texas didn't have to be made on a grill? I decided it was worth a try in the slow cooker. The marbling of a skirt steak or sirloin flap meat makes it a fine match for a very low simmer. You get to, pretty much, throw everything together in the cooker, too. Then you have plenty of time to make up guacamole or salsa while the meat is cooking.

Vegetable oil spray

2 to 2½ pounds (about 1 kg) skirt steak (inside or outside skirt), or sirloin flap, in 1 or more pieces, trimmed of excess fat, cut as needed to lay in the slow cooker

2 teaspoons (6 g) kosher salt or coarse sea salt

½ teaspoon ground cumin

1 large red onion, halved and sliced into ½-inch (1-cm) wide half-moons

Juice of 2 large limes

Juice of 1 large orange

1 tablespoon (15 ml) Tabasco chipotle sauce

2 red bell peppers

2 poblano chiles, or other fresh mild-to-medium green chiles

Warm flour tortillas, guacamole, one or more salsas, and lime wedges to squeeze over the meat, for accompaniments

① Generously spray the inside of the slow cooker with oil.

② Lay the skirt steaks side-by-side, or as close as you can get to that, in the bottom of the slow cooker. Sprinkle with the salt and cumin. Cover with the onion slices. In a small bowl, stir together the lime juice, orange juice, and Tabasco sauce. Pour the mixture evenly over the onions. Arrange the whole bell peppers and poblanos on top. Cover and cook on low for 7 to 8 hours, or 4 to 4½ hours on high.

③ Remove the steaks and vegetables from the slow cooker. Let the steaks sit covered with foil while you slice the peppers and chiles into thin strips. Toss them together with the onions.

④ With a knife at a slight diagonal, cut the steaks across the grain into thin finger-width strips. To serve, pile the steak strips and vegetable strips on a large platter, offer a napkin-lined basket of the warm tortillas, bowls of guacamole, and salsa. Spoon portions of the steak and vegetables into the tortillas, top with guacamole and salsa, fold up, and chow down.

SKIRT STEAK WITH CHIMICHURRI

YIELD: SERVES 6 | COOKING TIME: 7 TO 8 HOURS ON LOW, 4 TO 4½ HOURS ON HIGH, CAN BE HELD ON WARM FOR 1 HOUR

Chimichurri came north from Argentina and found a warm welcome throughout the state of Texas. The herbal combo of ingredients is the perfect match with hearty beef, with vinegar offering a tart counterpoint to rich skirt steak.

2 teaspoons (10 ml) extra-virgin olive oil

2 to 2½ pounds (about 1 kg) skirt steak (inside or outside skirt), or sirloin flap, in 1 or more pieces, trimmed of excess fat, cut as needed to lay in the slow cooker

2 to 3 teaspoons (10 to 15 g) Worcestershire sauce or Worcestershire powder

Kosher salt or coarse sea salt or smoked salt

CHIMICHURRI

¼ cup (60 ml) red wine vinegar

¼ cup (60 ml) water

1 teaspoon kosher salt or coarse sea salt

¾ cup (45 g) fresh flat-leaf parsley

½ cup (8 g) fresh cilantro

¼ cup (24 g) fresh mint

6 plump garlic cloves

½ teaspoon hot red chile flakes

½ cup (118 ml) extra-virgin olive oil

① Generously grease the inside of the slow cooker with oil.

② Lay the skirt steaks side-by-side, or as close as you can get to that, in the bottom of the slow cooker. Cover with Worcestershire sauce or powder, and add salt to taste. Cover and cook on low for 7 to 8 hours, or 4 to 4½ hours on high.

③ While the steaks cook, make the chimichurri. Combine the vinegar, water, and salt in a blender, and buzz a couple of times to dissolve the salt. Add the parsley, cilantro, mint, garlic, and chile flakes, and chop the herbs coarsely. With the blender running, pour in the oil to make a thin green emulsion. It can sit at room temperature for a couple of hours, but otherwise refrigerate covered until needed.

④ Remove the steaks from the slow cooker and let sit covered with foil for about 10 minutes.

⑤ With a knife at a slight diagonal, cut the steaks across the grain into finger-width strips. To serve, pile the steak strips on a platter and accompany with spoonfuls of chimichurri sauce. Any remaining "chimi" can be refrigerated for up to a week.

VIETNAMESE FAJITAS

YIELD: SERVES 4 TO 6 | COOKING TIME: 7 TO 8 HOURS ON LOW, CAN BE HELD ON WARM FOR 1 HOUR

The La family arrived in Houston from Vietnam in 1980 and began Kim Son, a café they built into the largest and most successful Vietnamese restaurant empire in the state. The family had the brilliant idea of calling the classic lemongrass beef dish, *bo nuong xa*, "Vietnamese fajitas." It was just the touch needed to make the oil executives and the urban cowboys of the era feel right at ease. Use of the Texa-fied name has spread to many other places serving the dish. While the flank steak preparation is typically grilled, using the slow cooker allows the very lean cut to cook evenly and to great tenderness.

1 tablespoon (15 ml) vegetable oil (divided)

1¼- to 1½-pound (570- to 680-g) flank steak

3 tablespoons (45 ml) soy sauce

1 tablespoon (15 ml) rice wine vinegar

1 stalk lemongrass, bruised with the side of chef's knife and then chopped

4 plump garlic cloves, minced

1 tablespoon (13 g) granulated sugar

1 teaspoon kosher salt or coarse sea salt

TABLE SAUCE

⅓ cup (80 ml) fish sauce

⅓ cup (66 g) sugar

1½ tablespoons (25 ml) rice wine vinegar

¾ cup (175 ml) water

Hot water

Eighteen 6-inch (15-cm) rice paper wrappers (bánh tráng)

1 large carrot, grated

½ medium cucumber, peeled, seeded and cut into matchsticks

½ cup (85 g) fresh pineapple slices, cut into matchsticks

½ cup (25 g) bean sprouts

⅓ cup (32 g) fresh mint leaves

⅓ cup (5 g) fresh cilantro leaves

1 large head Bibb or Boston leaf lettuce or ½ head iceberg lettuce, pulled into individual leaves

① Generously grease the inside of the slow cooker with about 1 teaspoon of the oil.

② Place the flank steak in the slow cooker. Combine in a small bowl the remaining oil, soy sauce, vinegar, lemongrass, garlic, sugar, and salt. Pour the mixture evenly over the flank steak. Cover and cook on the low heat setting for 7 to 8 hours, until the meat is very tender.

③ While the beef is cooking, prepare the sauce, combining the ingredients in a small bowl. Let the sauce sit at room temperature.

④ Prepare the rice paper wrappers up to approximately 2 hours ahead of time. Pour about 1 inch (2.5 cm) of hot water into a shallow 8- or 9-inch (20- or 23-cm) square baking dish. Soak the rice papers individually in hot water. Place them on a platter, slightly offset from each other so that they can be pulled apart. Cover with a damp towel until serving time.

⑤ Cut the steak into thin strips across the grain. Transfer to a platter. Accompany with the sauce, carrot, cucumber, pineapple, sprouts, mint, cilantro, and lettuce. Let everyone assemble their own "fajitas."

THE LA FAMILY, WHO ARRIVED IN HOUSTON FROM VIETNAM IN 1980, PRESIDE OVER THE MOST SUCCESSFUL VIETNAMESE RESTAURANT EMPIRE IN THE STATE. IT WAS THE LAS WHO CAME UP WITH THE BRILLIANT IDEA OF CALLING THE CLASSIC LEMONGRASS BEEF DISH, *BO NUONG XA,* "VIETNAMESE FAJITAS."

GROUND BEEF PICADILLO, SAN ANTONIO SISTER-IN-LAW STYLE

YIELD: SERVES 6 OR MORE | **COOKING TIME:** 2 TO 2½ HOURS ON HIGH, 4 TO 5 HOURS ON LOW, CAN BE HELD ON WARM FOR UP TO 2 HOURS

Long ago, I used to fancify what I considered Tex-Mex picadillo—with olives, and raisins, and nuts, and who knows what else. My San Antonio–born-and-bred sister-in-law, Rose Delgado Jamison, thought it was something of a travesty. She convinced me to go back to the basics, and I've never strayed again. Supremely good for tacos and Sloppy Joes of a sort, picadillo is more delicious than you might guess a ground beef mixture to be. Starting from freshly ground chuck helps give a big flavor boost. Picadillo can fill tacos, enchiladas, burritos, or tostadas, or be spooned onto a bun. I like a bowl of it late at night with some tortilla chips to scoop it up and a bottle of Cholula hot sauce on the side.

2 tablespoons (30 ml) vegetable oil (divided)

1 medium baking potato, peeled and chopped fine

1 large onion, minced

6 plump garlic cloves, minced

2 pounds (905 g) freshly ground beef chuck

1 tablespoon (8 g) unbleached all-purpose flour

1 teaspoon dried Mexican oregano or dried marjoram

1 teaspoon chili powder

½ teaspoon ground cumin

½ teaspoon kosher salt or coarse sea salt

½ cup (120 ml) low-sodium beef broth

¼ teaspoon Maggi sauce or 1 teaspoon soy sauce

① Grease the inside of the slow cooker with 1 teaspoon of the oil.

② Place the chopped potato in the slow cooker.

③ In a skillet, warm the rest of the oil over medium heat. Add the onion and garlic. Sauté for a couple of minutes until just beginning to soften. Add the meat and fry until it has lost its raw color. It does not need to be thoroughly cooked. Stir in the flour, oregano, chili powder, cumin, and salt. Scrape the mixture into the slow cooker. Pack down evenly. Pour broth and Maggi sauce over the top.

④ Cover and cook on the high heat setting for 2 to 2½ hours or on the low setting for 4 to 5 hours. The picadillo is ready when the potatoes have softened fully and melded with the meat. The liquid should be a bit thickened from the flour and potatoes. Serve hot in tortillas or taco shells, on soft burger buns, or simply plated.

DRUNKEN DESHEBRADA

YIELD: SERVES 6 | COOKING TIME: 4½ TO 5 HOURS ON HIGH, 9 TO 10 HOURS ON LOW

Deshebrada is classic shredded beef filling for tacos and enchiladas. If you'd really rather have sober beef, substitute low-sodium beef broth for the beer. It's quite a flexible preparation, and easy to make a day or two ahead of when you plan to serve it. Leftovers will keep for at least a couple of days.

Vegetable oil spray

2½-pound (1.1 kg) beef chuck roast

1 medium onion, chopped

3 plump garlic cloves, minced

1 bay leaf

1 beer (12 ounces, or 355 ml), preferably a Mexican lager, such as Bohemia

1 canned chipotle chile, chopped and 1 tablespoon (15 g) adobo sauce from the can

1 teaspoon kosher salt or coarse sea salt

① Generously spray the inside of the slow cooker with oil.

② Place the chuck roast in the slow cooker and top with the remaining ingredients. Cover and cook on the high heat setting for 4½ to 5 hours or low heat setting for 9 to 10 hours. The beef is ready when fall-apart tender.

③ Shred the meat with 2 forks or your fingers, discarding fat and the bay leaf. Serve hot as a filling for tacos or enchiladas.

BARBACOA

YIELD: SERVES 6 OR MORE | COOKING TIME: 11 TO 12 HOURS ON LOW, 5½ TO 6 HOURS ON HIGH, CAN BE HELD ON WARM FOR 2 HOURS

Barbacoa isn't just any old barbecue. Traditionally, the meat is *cabeza de vaca*, the head of a cow, especially popular in South Texas. The unctuous meat often fills breakfast tacos, but it is good any time of day wrapped in a tortilla and dotted with cilantro and minced onion. A home cook can make a version of this treat with a beef cheek, a cut you can nearly always find at a Mexican market. Beef cheek makes a perfect slow-cooker meat, because the low slow cooking yields beautifully shredded meat, with a flavor of an extra-beefy chuck roast.

Vegetable oil spray

4 to 4½ pounds (1.8 to 2 kg) beef cheek meat, trimmed of surface fat

2 teaspoons (6 g) kosher salt or coarse sea salt or smoked salt

2 teaspoons (4 g) coarsely ground black pepper

2 teaspoons (5 g) ground cumin

1 teaspoon dried crumbled Mexican oregano or dried marjoram

8 whole plump garlic cloves

2 bay leaves

1 lime, halved

½ cup (120 ml) low-sodium beef broth

Warm flour or corn tortillas, favorite salsa, minced onion, and chopped fresh cilantro, for accompaniments

① Generously spray the inside of the slow cooker with oil.

② Arrange the meat in the slow cooker and cover with the salt, pepper, cumin, oregano, garlic, and bay leaves. Squeeze the two halves of the lime over the meat and add the lime shells to the slow cooker. Pour the broth around the edges and cover. Cook on the low heat setting for 11 to 12 hours or on high for 5½ to 6 hours, until the meat is very tender and will shred easily.

③ Transfer the meat with tongs or a slotted spoon to a cutting board. When cool enough to handle, shred the meat into bite-size pieces with 2 forks or your fingers. Discard any fat or gristle. Pour a few tablespoons of the cooking liquid into the shredded meat. Adjust the seasoning, if needed.

④ Serve the barbacoa in tortillas, accompanied by salsa, onion, and cilantro. Heavenly.

CHILI GRAVY

YIELD: SERVES 6 OR MORE | COOKING TIME: 2 TO 2½ HOURS ON HIGH, 4 TO 5 HOURS ON LOW

"With the opening in 1897 of the first Tex-Mex restaurant, Marfa's Old Borunda Café, the culinary history of Texas emerged from the dark ages and entered the renaissance," according to *Texas Monthly* writer Richard West. Central to that glory is chili gravy, a deeply burnished blanket of comfort and joy, essential for slathering over Lone Star enchiladas and many other Tex-Mex dishes. I love to ladle it over Frito pies myself.

2 tablespoons (30 ml) vegetable oil or bacon drippings (divided)

1 medium onion, chopped fine

3 plump garlic cloves, minced

1 pound (455 g) chili-grind ground round or ground chuck

¼ cup plus 2 tablespoons (47 g) ground dried ancho chile

¼ cup plus 2 tablespoons (47 g) New Mexican red chile

1 tablespoon (9 g) masa harina

2 teaspoons (5 g) ground cumin

½ teaspoon dried Mexican oregano or dried marjoram

½ teaspoon kosher salt or coarse sea salt

3 cups (705 ml) low-sodium beef broth

½ teaspoon Maggi sauce or 2 teaspoons (10 ml) soy sauce

① Generously grease the inside of the slow cooker with about 1 teaspoon of the oil or drippings.

② Warm the remaining oil in a medium skillet over medium heat. Add the onion and garlic. Sauté for a couple of minutes until just beginning to soften. Add the beef and fry until it has lost its raw color, breaking it up well with a spatula while it cooks. The beef does not need to be thoroughly cooked. Stir in both chiles, masa harina, cumin, oregano, and salt. Scrape the mixture into the slow cooker. Pour the broth and Maggi sauce over, and stir together.

③ Cover and cook on the high heat setting for 2 to 2½ hours or on the low setting for 4 to 5 hours. The beef should be very tender and the sauce lightly thickened from the masa harina. Ladle over beef or cheese enchiladas, burritos, or other Tex-Mex dishes.

BEEF ENCHILADAS

YIELD: SERVES 6 | COOKING TIME: 3½ TO 4 HOURS ON LOW

Behold the Tex-Mex enchilada, a double helping of brawny beef, inside and over. You can fill these with either Picadillo San Antonio Sister-in-Law Style (page 82) or Drunken Deshebrada (page 83), but I also put a simple quicker mixture in this recipe that will taste fine under the blanket of cheese and Chili Gravy (page 85). If you have a choice, make these in an oval slow cooker. This version uses the tortillas laid flat rather than rolled around the filling, making them a little more El Paso–style than is traditional elsewhere in Texas. It's ultimately difficult to recognize their shape anyway, shrouded by all that chili and cheese.

FILLING

1½ pounds (680 g) ground chuck

1 small onion, chopped

¾ teaspoon kosher salt or coarse
   sea salt

½ teaspoon freshly ground
   black pepper

Vegetable oil spray

Chili Gravy (page 85)

1 dozen corn tortillas

1 pound (455 g) mild Cheddar
   or Colby longhorn cheese, grated

① Prepare the filling. In a medium skillet, cook the ground beef over medium heat until it has lost its raw color. Mix in the onion, salt, and pepper, and continue to cook until the meat is browned and the onion is tender.

② Generously spray the inside of the slow cooker with oil.

③ Spoon enough of the Chili Gravy into the bottom of the slow cooker to cover the bottom. Arrange a layer of 4 tortillas, tearing them if needed to cover evenly. Top with one-third of the remaining Chili Gravy and one-third of the cheese. Repeat layers twice more, ending with the cheese.

④ Cover and cook on the low heat setting for 3 to 3½ hours until bubbly with golden brown edges. Uncover and cook 30 minutes more. Serve piping hot scooped out in large, neat spoonfuls.

⨯ CHEESE ENCHILADAS WITH CHILI GRAVY ⨯

Build the enchiladas upward in similar fashion. Just leave out the beef filling and instead, increase the cheese by a half-pound (225 g). Add some finely chopped onion between the layers, too. These are my personal favorite. If you want to be really old-fashioned about them, use Velveeta as the cheese.

CARNE GUISADA

YIELD: SERVES 6 | COOKING TIME: 6 HOURS ON LOW, 3 TO 3½ HOURS ON HIGH, CAN BE HELD ON WARM FOR UP TO 2 HOURS

Carne guisada is a beef stew that also makes a superb taco filling. In fact, that's often the main use of it. This version is based on one I remember enjoying more than two decades ago at Güero's in Austin. That was before the restaurant moved to the bustling South Congress neighborhood and became a much-better-known sensation.

2 tablespoons (30 ml) vegetable oil (divided)

2½ pounds (about 1 kg) beef chuck roast or bottom round, in 1-inch (2.5-cm) cubes

1 teaspoon kosher salt or coarse sea salt, or more to taste

1 teaspoon freshly ground black pepper

3 tablespoons (24 g) unbleached all-purpose flour

12 ounces (1½ cups, or 355 ml) low-sodium beef broth, preferably, or low-sodium chicken broth

1 medium onion, chopped

3 celery stalks, chopped

1 or 2 fresh jalapeño or serrano chiles, minced

1 tablespoon (16 g) tomato paste

2 teaspoons (5 g) ground cumin

½ teaspoon chili powder

① Grease the inside of the slow cooker with about 1 teaspoon of the oil.

② Sprinkle the meat with the salt and pepper. Warm 1 tablespoon (15 ml) of the oil in a heavy medium or large skillet. When hot, add half of the beef pieces and sauté until all have lost their raw color. Sprinkle with half of the flour and continue cooking until the beef pieces are browned. Scrape the mixture into the slow cooker. Add the remaining oil to the skillet and repeat with the remaining beef and flour.

③ Pour the broth over the meat in the slow cooker. Add the remaining ingredients and stir together. Cover and cook on the low heat setting for approximately 6 hours, or on high for 3 to 3½ hours. Adjust the seasoning with additional salt and pepper, if needed. Serve hot as a taco filling or as a stew.

SAUCY BEEF FOR SANDWICHES

YIELD: SERVES 8 OR MORE | **COOKING TIME:** 10 HOURS ON LOW, 5 HOURS ON HIGH, CAN BE HELD ON WARM FOR 2 HOURS

You can Google "slow cooker BBQ beef sandwiches" and end up with some four zillion recipes, and most pretty much combine beef and a bottle of barbecue sauce. Let's try a little harder for Texas-style faux Q. This version will take you a few more minutes to put together, and it won't fool Aaron Franklin or John Mueller, but you'll end up with a luscious sandwich.

DRY RUB

1 tablespoon (15 g) smoked salt

1 tablespoon (15 g) packed brown sugar

1 tablespoon (7 g) smoked paprika

1 tablespoon (8 g) chili powder

1 tablespoon (6 g) ground black pepper

3-pound (1.4-kg) beef chuck roast, cut in 4 equal pieces

Vegetable oil spray

¼ cup (60 g) Worcestershire sauce

¼ cup (60 g) tomato-based barbecue sauce

1 tablespoon (15 ml) pickling liquid from a jar of pickled jalapeños, or white vinegar

1 teaspoon Maggi sauce or 2 teaspoons (10 ml) soy sauce

6 plump garlic cloves, sliced

8 kaiser rolls, onion rolls, or large hamburger buns

① Combine the dry rub ingredients in a large bowl. Add the beef pieces to the bowl and rub them with the dry spices.

② Generously spray the inside of the slow cooker with oil.

③ Transfer the beef to the slow cooker. In a bowl, combine the Worcestershire sauce, barbecue sauce, pickling liquid, Maggi sauce, and garlic. Pour the mixture over the beef. Cover and cook on the low heat setting for approximately 10 hours, or on high for 5 hours, until the beef is quite tender. Shred the beef in the slow cooker with 2 forks, stirring the beef together with the juices.

④ Spoon beef onto rolls and serve right away.

SLOPPY JOES

YIELD: SERVES 8 | COOKING TIME: 7 TO 8 HOURS ON LOW, 3½ TO 4 HOURS ON HIGH, CAN BE HELD ON WARM UP TO 2 HOURS

No, it's not just for kids. Even that arbiter of mid-century good culinary taste in Texas, Helen Corbitt, included Sloppy Joes in her book *Potluck*. Sloppy Joes can make great game day food, whether you are tailgating or watching at home. Make sure that you have sturdy plates—no cheapo paper numbers here—and decent napkins, and you're good to go. If you can't easily come by dill seed, it's okay to use dried dill instead. Either adds an interesting note to the ground beef mixture. If you're feeling a bit more adventuresome, ground goat meat makes an excellent substitution for the beef.

2 tablespoons (30 ml) bacon drippings or vegetable oil (divided)

1 medium onion, chopped fine

1 large celery stalk, chopped fine

4 plump garlic cloves, minced

2 pounds (905 g) lean ground beef

1 tablespoon (7 g) dill seed or 2 teaspoons (2 g) dried dill

1 teaspoon chili powder

1 teaspoon kosher salt or coarse sea salt

2 cans (8 ounces, or 225 g) tomato sauce (or 1 can, 15 ounces, or 425 g tomato sauce)

2 tablespoons (22 g) yellow mustard

2 tablespoons (28 ml) cider vinegar or white vinegar, or brine from a jar of dill pickles

1 or 2 tablespoons (15 to 30 g) packed brown sugar or turbinado sugar

1 tablespoon (15 g) Worcestershire sauce

½ teaspoon Maggi sauce or 1 teaspoon soy sauce

8 soft hamburger buns

① Grease the inside of the slow cooker with about 1 teaspoon of the bacon drippings.

② In a large skillet, warm the remaining bacon drippings over medium heat. Add the onion, celery, and garlic, and sauté for a couple of minutes until just beginning to soften. Add the ground beef, dill seed, chili powder, and salt, and fry until the beef has lost its raw color. It does not need to be thoroughly cooked. Break up any large pieces with a large wooden spoon or spatula as it cooks. Scrape the mixture into the slow cooker. Pack down evenly. Pour in the tomato sauce, mustard, vinegar, brown sugar, Worcestershire sauce, and Maggi sauce.

④ Cover and cook on the low heat setting for 7 to 8 hours or on high for 3½ to 4 hours.

⑤ Spoon Sloppy Joe mixture onto buns and serve.

SOUTHWESTERN MEAT LOAF

YIELD: SERVES 6 OR MORE | **COOKING TIME:** 3 TO 4 HOURS ON LOW

When I was living in Dallas long ago, friends used to invite me over for meat loaf. I never let on that I really didn't like meat loaf. Gradually, though, I came to appreciate it, and once the friends moved away, I surprised myself by making meat loaf just for me. When I got together with my husband, he told me it was among his very favorite dishes, especially for cold sandwiches after the initial hot dinner version. I perfected a version with these seasonings, but never considered making it in the slow cooker until I began to work on this book. It makes a very moist and tender meat loaf. Cut the round or oval loaf in slices or wedges, as you wish.

Vegetable oil spray

2 pounds (905 g) meat loaf mix
(1 pound [455 g] ground beef plus
½ [225 g] pound each ground veal
and ground pork)

2 large eggs, lightly beaten

3 tablespoons (42 g) unsalted butter

2 cups (320 g) chopped onion
(about 2 medium onions)

4 plump garlic cloves, minced

4 tablespoons (60 g) tomato-based
barbecue sauce, such as Stubb's
(divided)

1 tablespoon (15 g) Worcestershire
sauce

½ cup (25 g) dried panko bread crumbs

1 tablespoon (8 g) chili powder

1 teaspoon ground cumin

1½ teaspoons kosher salt or coarse
sea salt

½ teaspoon freshly ground
black pepper

¾ cup (3 ounces, or 85 g) shredded
Monterey Jack or pepper Jack cheese

① Generously spray the inside of the slow cooker with oil. Tear off two sheets of aluminum foil, at least 12 inches (30 cm) long. Lay the foil sheets in crisscross directions over each other, with foil extending at least partially up the inside of the slow cooker. Spray the foil liner with oil.

② Combine in a medium bowl the meat loaf mix and eggs. Working with your hands will be easiest.

③ Warm the butter in a medium skillet over medium heat. Add the onion and garlic and cook until translucent, about 5 minutes. Stir in 2 tablespoons (30 g) of the barbecue sauce, the Worcestershire sauce, bread crumbs, chili powder, cumin, salt, and pepper. Cook briefly, just until spices are fragrant. Set aside to cool briefly, then mix into the meat mixture.

④ Pat one-half of the meat loaf mixture into the bottom of the slow cooker. Sprinkle cheese over the meat, leaving a border of about ½ inch (1 cm) on all sides. Pat the rest of the meat over the cheese. Brush with the remaining 2 tablespoons of barbecue sauce. Cook the meat loaf on the low heat setting until tender with an internal temperature of 160°F (71°C).

⑤ Slice the meat loaf and serve, or save part of the loaf, refrigerate it, and make cold meat loaf sandwiches for another meal.

GERMAN MEATBALLS

So many cultures have a version of meatballs and gravy, one of the ultimate comfort foods. This version owes its heritage to the German families that settled in central Texas. If available at your supermarket, substitute two pounds of "meat loaf" mix for the individual three meats. The proportions are similar. Try the meatballs and their gravy over buttered noodles with a sauté of red cabbage on the side.

Vegetable oil spray

2 tablespoons (28 g) unsalted butter

1½ cups (240 g) finely chopped onion

1 pound (455 g) ground chuck

½ pound (225 g) ground pork

½ pound (225 g) ground veal

½ cup (40 g) uncooked
   quick-cooking oats

½ cup (120 ml) half-and-half

2 large eggs, lightly beaten

4 anchovies, mashed

3 tablespoons (12 g) chopped flat-leaf
   parsley (divided)

2 teaspoons (6 g) kosher salt or coarse
   sea salt

½ teaspoon freshly ground black pepper

⅛ teaspoon ground cloves

1 cup (235 ml) Gewürztraminer or other
   off-dry (not sweet) white wine

½ cup (120 ml) low-sodium beef
   or chicken broth

1 bay leaf

1 medium lemon, halved lengthwise
   and cut into very thin half-moons

2 tablespoons (17 g) small capers

Cooked wide egg noodles,
   for accompaniment

① Generously spray the inside of the slow cooker with oil.

② Warm the butter in a medium skillet over medium-low heat. Add the onions, cover and sweat the onions for about 5 minutes, until tender. Scrape the mixture into a mixing bowl. Add to it the ground meats, oats, half-and-half, eggs, anchovies, 2 tablespoons (8 g) parsley, and the salt, pepper, and cloves. Using your hands, mix together until well combined. Pinch off portions of the meat mixture and form into a dozen golf-ball size meatballs. Place them on a microwaveable plate and zap in the microwave on high heat for about 5 minutes until the meatballs have lost their raw color and have rendered some fat.

③ Transfer meatballs to the slow cooker. (Discard the rendered fat.) Add the wine, broth, bay leaf, lemon, and capers. Cover and cook for 4 to 5 hours on the low heat setting. Discard the bay leaf.

④ Serve over noodles with some of the cooking liquid. Garnish with the remaining 1 tablespoon of parsley.

5

PORK, GOAT, AND POULTRY

★ PORK, GOAT, AND POULTRY ★

RIBLETS WITH JEZEBEL SAUCE

YIELD: SERVES 5 TO 6 | COOKING TIME: 7 TO 8 HOURS ON LOW, 3½ TO 4 HOURS ON HIGH, PLUS A FEW EXTRA MINUTES OF BAKING TIME AT THE END

Jezebel is one sassy Southern lady, with sweet, hot, and slyly wicked tones. When I moved to Texas in 1978, she was poured ever so innocently over a block of cream cheese, just waiting to give me a piquant kick in the pants, when scooped up on a cracker. I wanted more, and I discovered she could be a muse to a ham or other pork, as she is here. Ketchup and soy sauce aren't traditional additions to the usual array of Jez's ingredients, but they work well to add depth to the sauce over the long cooking time. These make a hearty appetizer, too.

Vegetable oil spray

3-pound (1.4-kg) rack baby back ribs

1½ teaspoons kosher salt or coarse sea salt

1½ teaspoons freshly ground black pepper

JEZEBEL SAUCE

¾ cup (240 g) apple jelly

3 tablespoons (64 g) Creole or brown mustard

1 tablespoon (15 g) ketchup

2 teaspoons (10 ml) soy sauce

1 tablespoon (15 g) prepared horseradish, or more to taste

① Generously spray the inside of the slow cooker with oil. Spray the ribs on both sides with oil.

② Rub the salt and pepper over both sides of the ribs.

③ Make the Jezebel Sauce: Combine the apple jelly, mustard, ketchup, soy sauce, and enough horseradish to wake up your mouth. Brush it on the meatier side of the ribs.

④ Arrange the ribs in the slow cooker standing on edge, with the meatier side toward the sides of the crock insert. Bend the ribs lightly, as needed, so that they stand up pretty much in contact with the crock. Cover and cook on the low heat setting for 7 to 8 hours or 3½ to 4 hours on high, until quite tender and easily bendable between the bones, but not yet to the fall-off-the-bone stage. (The ribs can be cooled and refrigerated overnight, if you wish. Let sit out 30 minutes at room temperature before proceeding.)

⑤ Let the ribs cool for 10 to 30 minutes. Arrange an oven rack in the middle of the oven. Preheat the oven to 400°F (200°C, or gas mark 6). Spoon out the sauce in the bottom of the cooker into a small saucepan and reduce by about one-half. Cut the ribs into individual riblets.

⑥ Place the ribs on a baking sheet (preferably with a silicone liner for easy cleanup). Pour the sauce over the ribs. Bake 10 to 15 minutes, until the sauce is sticky and begins to caramelize on the ribs.

⑦ Eat up, with lots of napkins handy.

STUFFED PORK CHOPS WITH PAN SAUCE

YIELD: SERVES 4 OR MORE | COOKING TIME: 2 TO 3 HOURS ON LOW, CAN BE HELD ON WARM FOR 1 HOUR

The moist cooking of the slow cooker keeps this great country dish from becoming the least bit dry. A butcher can slice a pocket into each pork chop if you want to save a few minutes of prep time.

Vegetable oil spray

3 tablespoons (42 g) unsalted butter

½ medium onion, chopped fine

½ medium green bell pepper, chopped fine

1 celery stalk, chopped fine

⅓ cup (50 g) golden raisins

1 cup (120 g) cornbread crumbs or 2 crumbled corn muffins

2 teaspoons minced fresh sage

1 teaspoon Dijon mustard

½ teaspoon dried thyme

2 teaspoons (24 g) instant tapioca

½ cup low-sodium chicken broth

4 double-thick center-cut pork chops, about 12 ounces (340 g) each

Kosher salt or coarse sea salt

① Generously spray the inside of the slow cooker with oil.

② Warm the butter in a skillet over medium heat. Stir in the onion, bell pepper, and celery, and sauté 5 to 7 minutes, until tender. Scrape the mixture into a small bowl, and stir in the cornbread crumbs, sage, mustard, and thyme. Cool briefly.

③ Using a thin sharp knife, cut a pocket into each pork chop. Make a cut straight into the chop, from one of its sides, then move the knife back and forth as needed—without cutting through any of the other sides—to open up a sizable pocket inside each chop. Keep the knife's slit on the outer surface from 1 to 2 inches (2.5 to 5 cm) in length so that most of the filling stays in the chops. Stuff about one-quarter of the mixture into the pocket in each chop. If any of the stuffing doesn't fit, just transfer it to the bottom of the slow cooker where it can flavor the sauce. Add the tapioca and broth to the slow cooker.

④ Sprinkle salt all over the chops. Transfer them to the slow cooker, arranging them in one layer, if possible. Cover and cook on the low heat setting for 2 to 3 hours until tender. Serve hot with a spoonful of sauce over each chop.

DESCENDANTS OF PIGS BROUGHT BY THE SPANISH, WILD HOGS RANGED FREELY AROUND TEXAS DURING THE FRONTIER PERIOD AND PROVIDED SOME OF THE PORK THAT EARLY TEXANS ATE.

SMOKY PORK RIBS

YIELD: SERVES 4 | COOKING TIME: 7 TO 8 HOURS ON LOW, 3½ TO 4 HOURS ON HIGH, PLUS A FEW EXTRA MINUTES OF BROILING TIME AT THE END

As much as Texas barbecue means beef and its brisket, pork ribs are nearly as well loved. I have smoked a lot of ribs in my Pitts & Spitts pit over the years, but I don't always have the time or inclination to hang outdoors most of the day fussing with them. No serious aficionado will confuse these with real Q, but they make a pretty fine substitute. They are cooked in "dry" fashion, then brushed with your choice of barbecue sauce before a quick crisping under the broiler for the best texture.

Vegetable oil spray

3-pound (1.4-kg) rack baby back ribs

¼ cup (60 g) smoked salt, such as Maldon

¼ cup (28 g) smoked hot or mild Spanish paprika

1 tablespoon (25 g) turbinado sugar

1 teaspoon chili powder

1 teaspoon ground cumin

1 tablespoon (15 ml) cider vinegar or white vinegar

1 tablespoon (15 g) Worcestershire sauce

¾ cup (180 g) favorite barbecue sauce, such as Stubb's Smokey Mesquite

① Generously spray the inside of the slow cooker with oil. Spray the ribs on both sides with oil.

② Combine in a small bowl the salt, paprika, sugar, chili powder, and cumin. Rub the dry-spice mixture all over both sides of the ribs. Really pack it on.

③ Arrange the ribs in the slow cooker on their side, standing on edge, with the meatier side toward the side of the crock insert. Bend the ribs lightly, as needed, so that they stand up pretty much in contact with the crock. Drizzle the vinegar and then the Worcestershire sauce over the top and sides of the ribs. Cover and cook on the low heat setting for 7 to 8 hours or 3½ to 4 hours on high, until quite tender and easily bendable between the bones, but not yet to the fall-off-the-bone stage. (The ribs can be cooled and refrigerated overnight, if you wish. Let sit 30 minutes at room temperature before proceeding.)

④ Arrange an oven rack so that is about 6 inches (15 cm) away from your broiler's heating element. Turn on the broiler. Place the ribs on a baking sheet (preferably with a silicone liner for easy cleanup), bonier side up. Cut the rack in two sections if it is too long to fit. Brush with about one-third of the barbecue sauce. Broil for 1 to 3 minutes, watching the ribs, until the sauce begins to caramelize. With tongs, turn the ribs over and brush the meatier side with the remaining barbecue sauce. Return the baking sheet to the broiler and broil for 1 to 3 minutes more, until the sauce is gooey and sticky and caramelized in spots.

⑤ Transfer the ribs to a cutting board. Let stand for about 10 minutes and then slice into individual portions. Eat up, with lots of napkins handy.

SMOTHERED PORK LOIN WITH SWEET POTATOES AND ONIONS

YIELD: SERVES 6 | COOKING TIME: 4½ TO 5½ HOURS ON LOW, CAN BE HELD ON WARM FOR 1 HOUR

Get yourself a somewhat compact pork loin, one that's as thick as possible, rather than long and thin. It will cook through more evenly in the slow cooker. If you have an oval slow cooker, use it here. If you don't, and it turns out that your pork loin is too long to fit in a round slow cooker, slice off one end as needed and wedge it in beside the larger section.

2 large onions, cut in 8 wedges each

1 large (14 to 16 ounces) or 2 medium sweet potatoes, peeled and cut in 1-inch (2.5-cm) cubes

1½ teaspoons kosher salt or coarse sea salt, or more to taste

1½ teaspoons coarsely ground black pepper

¼ teaspoon cayenne pepper

3-pound (1.4-kg) pork loin roast

4 ounces (115 g) thick-sliced bacon, chopped

2 tablespoons (30 g) Worcestershire sauce

3 plump garlic cloves, slivered

2 teaspoons crumbled dried thyme

2 teaspoons crumbled dried sage

1 tablespoon (8 g) cornstarch

¼ cup (60 ml) low-sodium chicken broth or water

1. Generously spray the inside of the slow cooker with oil. Place the onion and sweet potato cubes in the slow cooker.

2. Combine the salt, pepper, and cayenne, and rub them all over the pork loin, patting the mixture into the surface well.

3. In a large cast-iron skillet or other large heavy pan, fry the bacon over medium-low heat, stirring occasionally. When bacon is crisp and well-browned, remove it with a slotted spoon. Drain the bacon on paper towels, and reserve it and the drippings.

4. Transfer the pork loin to the skillet, and raise the heat to medium. Brown the meat on all sides in the drippings. Transfer the pork to the slow cooker, fat-side up. Pour the Worcestershire sauce evenly over the pork. Scatter in garlic, thyme, and sage. In a small bowl, stir together the cornstarch with the broth and pour the mixture around the pork.

5. Cover and cook for 4½ to 5½ hours on low until pork loin is cooked through and still tender. Remove pork from the slow cooker with tongs and transfer it to a cutting board. Let it sit for 10 minutes uncovered. Arrange the vegetables on a platter. Slice pork and arrange it over or beside the vegetables. Spoon pan sauce over, scatter with bacon, and serve.

PORK ROAST WITH APPLES AND SAUERKRAUT

YIELD: SERVES 6 | COOKING TIME: 8 TO 9 HOURS ON LOW, 4 TO 5 HOURS ON HIGH

It's a long way from the Czech Republic to rural Texas, but the state has the largest population of Czechs outside of the homeland. Many emigrants found their way from regions of Moldavia and Bohemia, in the middle to late nineteenth century, settling in the triangle bounded by Houston, Dallas, and San Antonio. West, Caldwell, Praha, Ennis, and Shiner are just a few of the communities today with these roots. In culinary terms, Czechs have kept *kolaches*, the scrumptious filled pastries, and pork on the tables. Tangy apples and sauerkraut help balance the richness of a pork roast.

2 tablespoons (30 ml) vegetable oil (divided)

1½ teaspoons kosher salt or coarse sea salt

1 teaspoon freshly ground black pepper

1 teaspoon sweet paprika

4- to 4½-pound (1.8- to 2.1-kg) boneless pork shoulder roast, rolled and tied

¼ cup (60 ml) off-dry or dry white wine, such as Gewürztraminer

1 large onion, grated or finely chopped in a food processor

2 large Granny Smith apples, peeled, cored, and grated or finely chopped in a food processor

1 tablespoon (15 g) packed brown sugar

2 pounds (905 g) sauerkraut, drained

2 teaspoons caraway seeds

① Generously grease the inside of the slow cooker with 1 teaspoon of the oil.

② Stir together the salt, pepper, and paprika, and rub the seasoning all over the roast.

③ Warm the remaining oil in a heavy skillet over medium-high heat. Add the pork and brown on all sides. Transfer the pork to the slow cooker. Pour the wine into the skillet and deglaze the pan. Reserve.

④ Place the onion and apples over and around the roast. Sprinkle with brown sugar. Add sauerkraut and arrange it around and over. Pour the deglazed pan juices over the sauerkraut. Top with the caraway seeds. Cover and cook on the low heat setting for 8 to 9 hours or on high for 4 to 5 hours. The pork should be very tender, shredding easily.

⑤ Transfer the pork to a cutting board. Let it sit for about 10 minutes, then slice thickly. Accompany the pork with portions of the sauer-kraut mixture and serve right away.

PORK CARNITAS

YIELD: SERVES 6 | COOKING TIME: 4 TO 4½ HOURS ON HIGH

Yes, there's enough oil here for a greased pig race, but it's the cooking medium for a technique that's somewhere between out-and-out frying and oil-poaching. Do use fresh oil for this, since it needs to be used for a fairly lengthy amount of time. The "little meats" are truly delectable.

2 tablespoons (15 g) chili powder

1 tablespoon kosher salt or coarse sea salt

2 teaspoons garlic powder

2 teaspoons (5 g) ground cumin

3- to 3½-pound (1.4- to 1.6-kg) boneless pork butt, cut into 8 more or less equal chunks, trimming away major portions of fat

2 bay leaves

Approximately 2 cups (472 ml) vegetable oil

Guacamole or avocado slices, salsa or pico de gallo, and warm flour or corn tortillas, for accompaniments

① In a small bowl, combine the chili powder, salt, garlic powder, and cumin. Rub the dry-spice mixture over the pork butt pieces.

② Transfer the pork butt to the slow cooker, then add bay leaves, and pour in enough oil to cover the pieces. Cover and cook on the high heat setting for 4 to 4½ hours until pork is very tender and will shred easily. Transfer the pork to a cutting board. When cool enough to handle, shred the pork with 2 forks or your fingers into bite-size shreds.

③ The pork can be served right away, or made to this point a day ahead, then reheated on a baking sheet under the broiler to develop some crispy edges. Discard the oil when it has cooled.

④ Serve the carnitas warm with your choice of accompaniments.

BRAISED HAM WITH JALAPEÑO JELLY GLAZE

YIELD: SERVES 8 TO 10 | COOKING TIME: 7½ TO 8½ HOURS ON LOW, CAN BE HELD FOR 2 HOURS ON WARM

Salty and sweet, with a little heat. Count me in.

Vegetable oil spray

6- to 7-pound (2.7 to 3.2-kg) cured ham

½ cup (120 ml) orange juice, fresh or from concentrate

½ cup (160 g) jalapeño jelly or jam, warmed

① Generously spray the inside of the slow cooker with oil.

② Using a sharp knife, remove any rind or skin from the ham. Cut away all but about ½ inch (1 cm) of the layer of fat. Score a diamond pattern in the top and sides of the ham, making crisscross cuts about an inch (2.5 cm) apart.

③ Transfer the ham to the slow cooker, a fat-side up. Pour the orange juice over the ham. Cover and cook the ham for 6 to 7 hours on the low heat setting.

④ With a basting bulb or a long-handled spoon, pour some of the liquid from the bottom of the slow cooker over the ham. Brush the jalapeño jelly over it. Cover again and cook for 1 more hour. Uncover and cook without the lid for about 30 minutes to dry out the jelly glaze somewhat.

⑤ Transfer the ham to a cutting board and let it sit for 15 to 30 minutes. Slice across the grain of the meat into thin pieces and serve. If you wish, degrease the liquid from the slow cooker and pour some of it over the ham slices too.

COCHINITA PIBIL

YIELD: SERVES 8 OR MORE | COOKING TIME: 8 TO 9 HOURS ON LOW, 4 TO 4½ HOURS ON HIGH, CAN BE HELD ON WARM FOR 2 HOURS

One of the glories of the Yucatán originally, where it is cooked in smoldering earthen pits, this can be called, arguably, the most popular kind of pulled pork in Texas. *Cochinita pibil* comes in a pretty handsome package too, all wrapped up in banana leaves. This is a great recipe for prepping and marinating overnight before cooking. The meat just gets better with a long soak in the spices. The quantity of habanero hot sauce is enough to give a hint of the incendiary chile's perfumy flavor but not enough to blast your taste buds. Add a bit more if you wish.

Vegetable oil spray

2 to 4 banana leaves

4- to 4½-pound (1.8 to 2.1-kg) boneless pork butt

¼ cup (60 ml) orange juice, fresh or from concentrate

2 tablespoons (30 ml) fresh lime juice

1 tablespoon (15 ml) white vinegar or cider vinegar

2 teaspoons (10 ml) habanero hot sauce or more to taste

2 tablespoons (16 g) chopped achiote paste

1 teaspoon crumbled dried Mexican oregano or marjoram

1 teaspoon ground allspice

1 teaspoon kosher salt or coarse sea salt

6 plump garlic cloves

3 bay leaves

Quick Pickled Onions (right) and warm corn tortillas, as accompaniments

① Spray the inside of the slow cooker with oil. Line it with 2 or 3 banana leaves, enough to cover the inside, with several inches of leaves flopping over the top sides of the cooker. You'll be wrapping the pork up like a present. Place the pork in the cooker.

② Combine the remaining ingredients in a food processor and process until you have a smooth thick paste. Spoon the paste over the pork butt, using your hands as needed to cover it all in the paste. Fold banana leaves over the top of the meat, covering as much of it as possible.

× QUICK PICKLED ONIONS ×

Make these while the meat cooks or prepare them a day or two ahead. Thinly slice 1 medium purple onion. Place onion slices in a small bowl and cover with very cold water. Let the mixture sit for 15 to 20 minutes, then pour off the water. Sprinkle onion slices with a pinch or two of kosher salt or coarse sea salt. Add 2 tablespoons (30 ml) of orange juice, fresh or from concentrate, 2 tablespoons (30 ml) of fresh lime juice, and 1 teaspoon of olive oil to the onion. Refrigerate the onions until ready to serve.

3. Cover and cook on the low heat setting for 8 to 9 hours, or 4 to 4½ hours on high, until fork-tender and easy to shred. (Test by unwrapping just a small bit and checking with a fork.) Using large tongs or a spatula, transfer the pork to a cutting board or rimmed baking sheet. Save a few tablespoons of the meat juices from the bottom of the slow cooker. When cool enough to handle, pull the meat apart with 2 forks or your fingers into bite-size shreds, discarding pieces of fat. Mix the reserved meat juices with the meat.

4. Transfer to a platter and serve. If you have extra banana leaves, you can arrange the pork on them. Accompany with Quick Pickled Onions (left) and warm corn tortillas.

ORIGINALLY A MEXICAN DISH FROM YUCATÁN, WHERE IT IS COOKED IN SMOLDERING EARTHEN PITS, COCHINITA PIBIL NOWADAYS IS ARGUABLY THE MOST POPULAR KIND OF PULLED PORK IN TEXAS.

HAM LOAF

YIELD: SERVES 6 OR MORE | COOKING TIME: 3 TO 4 HOURS ON LOW

Ground ham preparations, such as salads or a loaf like this, are dishes I always associate with cooks of German extraction. This is just as scrumptious as a great meat loaf. If you'd like to try another Texan-inspired glaze, skip the mustard–turbinado sugar combo on top and brush this with the Jezebel Sauce from page 96. This is superb made from leftovers of Braised Ham with Jalapeño Jelly Glaze, page 103.

Vegetable oil spray

3 tablespoons (42 g) unsalted butter

1½ cups (240 g) chopped onion

¾ cup (90 g) minced celery

1 pound (455 g) ground ham

1 pound (455 g) ground pork

3 large eggs, lightly beaten

1 tablespoon (15 g) Worcestershire sauce

2 tablespoons (30 g) brown mustard (divided)

2 teaspoons (10 ml) soy sauce (divided)

2 teaspoons (10 g) prepared horseradish

1 teaspoon ground coriander

1½ teaspoons kosher salt or coarse sea salt

½ teaspoon freshly ground black pepper

¾ cup (90 g) soft bread crumbs

1 tablespoon (25 g) turbinado sugar

① Generously spray the inside of the slow cooker with oil. Tear off two sheets of aluminum foil, at least 12 inches (30 cm) long. Lay the foil sheets in crisscross directions over each other, with foil extending at least partially up the inside of the slow cooker. Spray the foil liner with oil.

② Warm the butter in a medium skillet over medium heat. Add the onion and celery. Cook until tender, about 8 minutes. Set aside to cool briefly.

③ Combine in a medium bowl the ground ham, ground pork, and eggs. Working with your hands will be easiest. Add the cooled onion-celery mixture, the Worcestershire sauce, 1 tablespoon (15 g) of mustard, 1½ teaspoons of the soy sauce, the horseradish, coriander, salt, pepper, and bread crumbs.

④ Pat the ham loaf mixture into the bottom of the slow cooker. Combine the remaining 1 tablespoon of mustard and ½ teaspoon soy sauce and brush over the loaf. Sprinkle evenly with turbinado sugar. Cook the ham loaf on the low heat setting until tender with an internal temperature of about 160°F (71°C), approximately 3 to 4 hours. Using the foil, lift out the loaf to a platter. (It will drip some juice.) Let sit for 10 to 15 minutes at room temperature.

⑤ Serve the ham loaf hot or chilled, in thick slices.

BRATS AND KRAUT

YIELD: SERVES 6 OR MORE | COOKING TIME: 2½ TO 3½ HOURS ON LOW, CAN BE HELD ON WARM FOR SEVERAL HOURS

Brats are the quintessential football food, whether tailgating or at home in the TV room. But heck, they are perfect for cheering on the Spurs or Mavericks and the Rangers and Astros, too. Just leave the brats and kraut in the slow cooker and let everyone help themselves. Don't forget the buns or rolls to turn them into sumptuous sandwiches. Serve more mustard on the side.

1 tablespoon plus 1 teaspoon (20 ml) vegetable oil (divided)

12 ounces (340 g) sauerkraut, drained

1 large onion, sliced in half and then cut into thin half-moons

1 dozen uncooked (fresh) bratwurst

¼ cup (84 g) coarse-ground hearty mustard

1 tablespoon (15 g) packed brown sugar

1 tablespoon plus 1 teaspoon (20 ml) soy sauce or 2 teaspoons (10 ml) Maggi sauce

½ teaspoon caraway seeds

1 beer (12 ounces, or 355 ml), preferably a lager such as Shiner Premium

Sturdy buns or rolls, split

① Grease the inside of the slow cooker with about 1 teaspoon of the oil. Place sauerkraut in the slow cooker.

② Warm the rest of the oil in a medium skillet over medium heat. Add the onion and cook until translucent, about 5 minutes. Scrape onion into the slow cooker. Nestle the brats over the onions and kraut. Add the mustard, brown sugar, soy sauce, caraway seeds, and beer. Cover and cook for 2½ to 3½ hours on low.

③ With tongs, serve a brat and some of the kraut mixture on a bun, and repeat.

SAUSAGE WITH GREEN TOMATO CHOWCHOW

YIELD: SERVES 6 OR MORE | COOKING TIME: 2 TO 3 HOURS ON LOW, CAN BE HELD ON WARM FOR 2 HOURS

Tangy sauerkraut pairs with full-bodied bratwurst, as in the previous recipe. In this case, richly flavored kielbasa or other Polish sausage mates with a tart, green tomato relish. While people think about green tomatoes at the end of the growing season, they can be picked any time. Farmers' market vendors often have a stash of them. If you already have chowchow or can pick up a jar of it at a market or grocery store, you can be halfway there.

CHOWCHOW

1 pound (455 g) green tomatoes

½ head white cabbage or about
    8 ounces (225 g) cauliflower florets

1 medium red bell pepper, chopped
    roughly

2 to 3 fresh jalapeños, seeded and
    chopped roughly

1 cup white vinegar

¾ cup (150 g) granulated sugar

1 tablespoon pickling spice

2 teaspoons (6 g) kosher salt or coarse
    sea salt

2 teaspoons (8 g) yellow mustard seeds

Vegetable oil spray

2½ pounds (about 1 kg) kielbasa
    or other Polish sausage, cut into
    2- to 3-inch (5- to 7.5-cm) sections

¼ cup (60 g) Worcestershire sauce

① To prepare the chowchow, finely chop the tomatoes, cabbage, bell pepper, and jalapeños in a food processor, in batches if necessary. Stop short of pureeing the mixture. Transfer to a saucepan, and add the remaining ingredients. Bring the mixture to a rolling boil over high heat, then reduce the heat to a simmer and continue cooking until the liquid evaporates but the mixture is still moist, probably about 25 minutes. Let the chowchow cool to room temperature, then refrigerate it until needed.

② Generously spray the inside of the slow cooker with oil.

③ Arrange the sausages in the slow cooker, then pour the Worcestershire sauce over them. Cover and cook for 2 to 3 hours on low, until sausages are tender and cooked through.

④ Serve the sausages with spoonfuls of chowchow, chilled or at room temperature, on the side.

CHICKEN BREASTS WITH CHIPOTLE CREAM

YIELD: SERVES 6 | COOKING TIME: 2½ TO 3 HOURS ON LOW

The boneless skinless chicken breast that we all want for convenience needs a little special treatment to show off its best side. Breasts need to be enveloped in a sauce while cooking to keep them moist. The added benefit is that the chicken will flavor the sauce, too, which more or less makes itself. You don't want to overwhelm the creamy base of the sauce with too much chipotle, but you want enough for your mouth to dance a little two-step.

Vegetable oil spray

Six 5- to 7-ounce boneless skinless chicken breasts

½ teaspoon kosher salt or coarse sea salt, or more to taste

Freshly ground black pepper

1 cup grated Parmesan cheese or Mozzarella Company Montasio cheese

1 chipotle chile, minced, plus 2 tablespoons (30 g) of adobo sauce from the can

1 cup heavy cream

6 tablespoons (84 g) unsalted butter, cut in 6 pieces

2 tablespoons (2 g) minced cilantro, for garnish

① Generously spray the inside of the slow cooker with oil.

② Arrange the chicken breasts in the bottom of the slow cooker. Sprinkle with the salt and a few grinds of pepper. Top with the Parmesan, scatter the chipotle and adobo, pour in the cream, and dot with the butter. Cover and cook on low for 2½ to 3 hours.

③ Spoon out the chicken breasts and place them on a platter. Pour the sauce into a blender and give it a whirl or two, until silky. Pour spoonfuls of sauce over each portion. Sprinkle with cilantro and serve.

NO GOAT IS GOING
TO FIT IN A SLOW
COOKER, BUT YOU
CAN FIND A PORTION
OF A YOUNG GOAT
OR KID IN MANY
MEXICAN MARKETS
THESE DAYS, AND
AT SOME FARMERS'
MARKETS.

CABRITO BIRRIA

YIELD: SERVES 6 OR MORE | COOKING TIME: 6 TO 7 HOURS ON LOW, CAN BE HELD ON WARM FOR SEVERAL MORE HOURS

Goat was among the original Texas barbecue meats, and it continues to be immortalized in central Texas at the Brady World Championship BBQ Goat Cook-Off. If you've never tried the meat, it's like the offspring of a cow and a pig. No goat is going to fit in a slow cooker, but you can find a portion of a young goat or kid in many Mexican markets these days, and at some farmers' markets. Windy Hill Farm in Boerne hits farmers' markets around the Austin area with its certified organic Boer goat meat. As with the slow heat of a barbecue fire, the moist low temperature of the slow cooker is a pretty much perfect match for the kid. Here, the meat is seasoned with a chile paste mixture in the braised Mexican style, *birria*. If you happen to come across a rack or two of young goat ribs, they can be cooked in similar fashion. Leftover meat makes scrumptious tacos. You'll understand why Texas troubadour Guy Clark wrote and sang, "I know a man that cooks cabrito/ It must be against the law . . ."

Vegetable oil spray

10 plump garlic cloves

¼ cup ground dried ancho chile

2 teaspoons (5 g) ground cumin

2 teaspoons (6 g) kosher salt or coarse
   sea salt

1 teaspoon coarsely ground
   black pepper

¼ cup (60 ml) water

1 tablespoon (15 ml) vegetable oil

1 tablespoon (15 ml) cider vinegar
   or white vinegar

1 pound (455 g) red potatoes, unpeeled,
   cut in ½-inch (1-cm) thick slices

3-pound (1.4 kg) young goat shoulder
   or rump roast

1 can (14 to 15 ounces, or 425 g) diced
   tomatoes with juice

Fresh cilantro leaves, chopped onion,
   and lime wedges, as accompaniment

① Generously spray the inside of the slow cooker with oil.

② Using a food processor with the motor running, drop the garlic cloves into the feed tube 1 or 2 at a time, letting each be minced fully before adding more. Stop the processor and add to it the ancho chile, cumin, salt, pepper, water, oil, and vinegar.

③ Arrange the potato slices in the bottom of the slow cooker. Top with the shoulder. Scoop the seasoning paste out of the food processor and rub it all around the visible surfaces of the meat. Pour the tomatoes and juice over all. Cover and cook for 6 to 7 hours on the low heat setting, until fall-apart tender.

④ Remove the roast to a work surface. When cool enough to handle, pull the meat into large shards, discarding fat and bone. Pile the meat on a platter or shallow baking dish. With a slotted spoon, scoop out the potatoes and arrange beside the meat. Cover with foil.

⑤ Skim fat from the surface of the cooking liquid in the slow cooker. Transfer cooking liquid to a saucepan and reduce the mixture over high heat by about one-half.

⑥ Arrange the meat and potatoes in deep plates or shallow bowls. Ladle some of the pan sauce over each. Scatter each portion with cilantro and onion, and tuck a lime wedge into each. Serve right away.

MARGARITA-GLAZED CHICKEN BREASTS

YIELD: SERVES 6 | COOKING TIME: 2½ TO 3 HOURS ON LOW

When cooking boneless skinless chicken breasts, you will have best results using the low heat setting. High tends to be too drying for the lean and tender poultry. After their time in the slow cooker, use the broiler to get a nice and sticky glaze on the breasts, a texture contrast to the silky meat.

1 tablespoon (15 ml) olive oil (divided)

Six 5- to 7-ounce (140- to 196-g) boneless skinless chicken breasts

1 teaspoon kosher salt or coarse sea salt

Freshly ground black pepper

1 can (3 ounces, or 85 g) frozen orange juice concentrate, thawed (divided)

Zest and juice of 1 medium lime plus juice of 2 more medium limes

¼ cup low-sodium chicken broth

¼ cup silver or gold tequila

① Grease the inside of the slow cooker with about 1 teaspoon of the oil.

② Arrange the chicken breasts in the bottom of the slow cooker. Sprinkle with the salt and a few grinds of pepper. Top with the rest of the olive oil, two-thirds of the orange juice concentrate, lime zest and juice, broth, and tequila. Cover and cook on low for 2½ to 3 hours.

③ Turn on the broiler.

④ Place chicken breasts on a rimmed baking sheet. Brush each with a portion of the remaining orange juice concentrate. Run under the broiler for 2 to 3 minutes, until glaze is sticky and browned in a few spots.

⑤ Give it all a good stir, then dish out the chicken breasts with spoonfuls of sauce for each portion.

× CHICKEN FAJITAS ×

This recipe makes really good chicken to wrap in warm flour tortillas. Slice the breasts across the grain and pile the chicken strips onto a platter with guacamole and salsa or pico de gallo.

CHICKEN TINGA

YIELD: SERVES 6 TO 8 | COOKING TIME: 2½ TO 3 HOURS ON LOW

A robust cross between a stew and a filling, tinga comes from Puebla, Mexico, and it incorporates spicy, sweet, smoky, and savory flavors. Traditional versions call for the roasting of tomatoes or tomatillos before pureeing. To keep the amount of work down when prepping this for the slow cooker, I use roasted canned tomatoes, such as Muir Glen, and smoky chipotle chiles.

Vegetable oil spray

2 pounds (905 g) boneless skinless chicken thighs or breasts, or a combination

½ pound (225 g) bulk Mexican chorizo

1 small onion, chopped fine

2 teaspoons (2 g) crumbled dried Mexican oregano or marjoram

2 bay leaves

1 can (15 ounces, or 425 g) roasted diced tomatoes with juice

2 canned chipotle chiles and 2 teaspoons (10 g) adobo sauce from the can

4 plump garlic cloves

2 tablespoons (30 ml) cider vinegar or white vinegar

1 teaspoon kosher salt or coarse sea salt

Soft corn tortillas, avocado slices or chunks, cilantro leaves, queso fresco, crema, pico de gallo, for accompaniments

① Generously spray the inside of the slow cooker with oil. Place chicken in bottom of cooker.

② Spray a medium skillet with oil. Warm over medium-high heat and add the chorizo and fry it until it begins to release oil. Reduce the heat to medium and add to the skillet the onion, oregano, and bay leaves. Cook about 5 minutes until the chorizo is browned in spots and the onion is soft. Scrape the mixture into the slow cooker, spreading it over the chicken.

③ Puree in a blender the tomatoes, chiles and sauce, garlic, vinegar, and salt. Pour the mixture into the cooker. Cover and cook on low for 2½ to 3 hours until stew-like. Discard the bay leaves.

④ Serve with or in corn tortillas, and top with your choice of one or more garnishes.

"ROAST" FIRE BIRD

YIELD: SERVES 4 | COOKING TIME: 4 TO 5 HOURS ON LOW

Rubbing a barbecue dry-spice mixture over and under the skin of a chicken, surprisingly to me, does not result in bold flavoring when using a slow cooker. Instead, I found that a moist seasoning paste, also sometimes used in barbecue, is more successful. The steamy cooking environment allows the flavoring to sink right down to the bone. Prepared in a slow cooker, a chicken will not develop a crisp skin, so you may want to discard it before eating the bird. However, keeping the skin on during the cooking is a must, as it adds flavor, helps hold the spice paste in place, and keeps the chicken extra moist while it is cooking. An oval-shaped slow cooker will work best for this recipe.

1½ tablespoons (21 g) bacon drippings or unsalted butter (divided)

1½ tablespoons (15 g) minced garlic

1 tablespoon (8 g) chili powder

2 teaspoons (6 g) kosher salt or coarse sea salt

2 teaspoons (10 g) Worcestershire sauce

2 teaspoons soy sauce

3½- to 4-pound (1.6- to 1.8-kg) whole chicken

① Generously grease the inside of the slow cooker with drippings.

② In a small skillet, warm the bacon drippings over medium heat. Add the garlic and sauté for about 3 minutes, stirring until tender. Stir in the chili powder and cook for another minute until fragrant. Remove from the heat and stir in the salt and Worcestershire sauce. Let cool briefly.

③ Massage the chicken with about one-third of the seasoning paste, working the mixture as far as possible under the skin without tearing it. Cover the chicken well with more of the paste, massage it inside and out, and over and under the skin.

④ Transfer the chicken breast-side down to the slow cooker. Cover and cook for 4 to 5 hours on low until an instant-read thermometer, stuck in the thigh, reaches 165°F (74°C).

⑤ Transfer the chicken to a carving board and let it sit for 10 minutes. Carve the chicken and serve.

KING RANCH CHICKEN CASSEROLE

YIELD: SERVES 6 TO 8 | COOKING TIME: APPROXIMATELY 4 HOURS ON LOW

The famed South Texas King Ranch is known for almost everything except chicken. Somehow though, its name found itself attached to this creamy iconic casserole with mostly mystery behind its history. You can count on it being put together in big-as-the-King-Ranch style. The not particularly attractive—but deeply satisfying—dish bears a resemblance to the flat-style enchilada casseroles made in far west Texas and next door in New Mexico. The dish *Texas Monthly* referred to as "Lord of the Potluck" is a staple today at Whole Foods prepared food counters, school cafeterias, and surely at ninety-nine out of every one hundred Lone Star potlucks. My stepdaughter, Heather, made a scrumptious version for my late husband during every visit.

Vegetable oil spray

3 to 4 cups (420 to 560 g) shredded or chopped, roasted or poached chicken

1 medium onion, chopped

6 ounces (168 g) thin-sliced button mushrooms

½ medium green bell pepper, chopped

1 garlic clove, minced

1 teaspoon chili powder

1 teaspoon salt

1 can (12 ounces, or 355 ml) evaporated milk

1 can (10 ounces, or 280 g) diced tomatoes and green chiles, such as Ro-Tel, undrained

1½ cups (6 ounces, or 168 g) shredded medium Cheddar cheese

1½ cups (6 ounces, or 168 g) shredded Jack cheese

12 6-inch (15 cm) corn tortillas

Crumbled tortilla chips, sliced scallions, or chopped fresh cilantro for garnishes, optional

① Generously spray the inside of the slow cooker with oil.

② Mix together in a large bowl the chicken, onion, mushrooms, bell pepper, garlic, chili powder, salt, evaporated milk, and tomatoes with chiles.

③ Spoon enough of the chicken-and-sauce mixture into the slow cooker to cover the bottom. Arrange a layer of 4 tortillas, tearing them if needed to cover evenly. Top with one-third of the remaining chicken-and-sauce mixture and one-half of the cheeses. Repeat layers once more, ending with the cheeses.

④ Cover and cook on the low heat setting for approximately 3½ hours until bubbly with golden brown edges. Uncover and cook 30 minutes more. Top the casserole or individual portions of it with tortilla chips for more crunch, or scallions or cilantro for more color. Serve piping hot scooped out in large neat spoonfuls.

CHICKEN SPAGHETTI

YIELD: SERVES 6 | COOKING TIME: 2 TO 2½ HOURS ON LOW

This one's a hot mess, kind of like Sue Ellen Ewing in the early years of the old *Dallas* TV series. A longtime staple, found in regional cookbooks since at least the late 1940s, chicken spaghetti is still a worthy stalwart, but nothing an Italian would recognize. I've stripped out the cans of soup usually called for to get back to real ingredients. Unlike the previous King Ranch casserole, chicken spaghetti comes out best starting with uncooked chicken. Don't skimp on the olives, which provide an important spark of tanginess to the otherwise creamy casserole.

12 ounces (340 g) spaghetti

4 slices thick-cut bacon, chopped

2 tablespoons (28 g) unsalted butter

1 large onion, chopped

1 cup minced fresh button mushrooms (10 to 12 medium)

2 large celery stalks, chopped

3 plump garlic cloves, minced

3 tablespoons (24 g) unbleached all-purpose flour

1½ teaspoons chili powder

1 cup (235 ml) low-sodium chicken broth

1 cup (235 ml) half-and-half

1½ teaspoons Worcestershire sauce

¾ teaspoon kosher salt or coarse sea salt

Vegetable oil spray

1 pound (455 g) uncooked, boneless, skinless chicken breast tenders or thighs, or a combination

½ cup (50 g) sliced pimento-stuffed olives

1½ cups (6 ounces, or 168 g) shredded medium Cheddar cheese (divided)

① Warm a large pot of salted water over high heat. Cook the spaghetti in the water until it is limp but very al dente, softening on the outside but still with a core of resistance at its center. Drain.

② While the spaghetti cooks, make the sauce mixture. Fry the bacon in a high-sided skillet or wide saucepan over medium-low heat until browned and crisp. With a slotted spoon, scoop out the bacon, and drain it on paper towels. Melt the butter in the bacon drippings and turn the heat up to medium. Add the onion, mushrooms, celery, and garlic to the skillet and cook down until all the vegetables are limp but still moist, 5 to 7 minutes. Stir in the flour and chili powder and, when incorporated, pour in the broth, half-and-half, Worcestershire sauce, and salt, and cook about 5 minutes more until lightly thickened.

③ Generously spray the inside of the slow cooker with oil. Place the chicken in the bottom of the slow cooker. Spoon the spaghetti over the chicken and then scatter on half of the cheese and the olives. Pour the sauce over and then top with the remaining cheese.

④ Cover and cook for 2 to 2½ hours on the low heat setting, until the chicken is cooked through and the mixture is cooked down and blended together. The chicken should pull apart into tender shreds. Serve piping hot, scooped out with a large spoon and fork, for best maneuvering.

CHICKEN SPAGHETTI HAS BEEN A STAPLE IN TEXAS COOKBOOKS SINCE AT LEAST THE 1940s. IT'S A WORTHY STALWART, BUT NOTHING AN ITALIAN WOULD RECOGNIZE.

GRANDMA'S CHICKEN AND DUMPLINGS

YIELD: SERVES 6 OR MORE | COOKING TIME: 3½ TO 4 HOURS ON LOW, WITH ABOUT 30 MINUTES ON HIGH

One of the great American stews, in essence. I lived in Dallas in the late 1970s, when there was just one café associated with the farmers' market on the south, then-scruffy, fringes of downtown. The little homey restaurant served chicken and dumplings, as I recall, only one day each week. I didn't work far from there, so I would try to get there at least once every few weeks on the assigned day.

Vegetable oil spray

CHICKEN

2 tablespoons (16 g) unbleached all-purpose flour

1 cup (235 ml) low-sodium chicken broth

2 tablespoons (60 ml) dry white wine, optional

2 pounds (905 g) boneless skinless chicken breasts, cut into cubes of about 1½ inches (3.5 cm)

1 large onion, chopped

2 medium carrots, chopped

3 plump garlic cloves, minced

1 bay leaf

1 teaspoon dried thyme

DUMPLINGS

1 cup (125 g) unbleached all-purpose flour

1¼ teaspoons baking powder

Scant ½ teaspoon kosher salt or coarse sea salt

¼ teaspoon dried thyme

½ cup (120 ml) half-and-half or whole milk

2 tablespoons (1 ounce, or 28 g) unsalted butter

FOR THE CHICKEN

① Generously spray the inside of the slow cooker with oil.

② Whisk together in the slow cooker the flour and several tablespoons of the broth. Pour in the remaining broth, continuing to whisk. Add the optional wine and then the remaining chicken ingredients.

③ Cover and cook on the low heat setting for 3½ to 4 hours. The chicken pieces and vegetables should be tender.

FOR THE DUMPLINGS

① While the chicken is cooking, prepare the dumplings. Stir together the flour, baking powder, salt, and thyme in a medium bowl. Heat together in a small saucepan the half-and-half and butter until small bubbles just break at the edge. Pour the warm liquid into the dry ingredients, and stir quickly until a soft dough just holds together. Quickly form the dough into a dozen balls.

ASSEMBLY

① Turn the slow cooker to high.

② Drop dumplings gently into the simmering liquid. Cover the slow cooker again and cook for approximately 30 more minutes, until the dumplings are biscuit-like and tender. Serve hot in large shallow bowls.

"QUICK" POSOLE

YIELD: SERVES 6 AS A MAIN DISH, MORE AS A SIDE | COOKING TIME: 2 TO 2½ HOURS ON HIGH, OR 6 TO 8 HOURS ON LOW

Posole, the Texican version of hominy, usually starts from a dried or frozen, lime-treated corn. It gets a quite long cooking process to become delectably tender-chewy. You can actually use commonly found canned hominy to make a posole-like dish and, even in a slow cooker, you can speed up the process while still developing a fairly deep flavor. A couple of chicken thighs give a bit of a meaty quality without the time needed for the more traditional pork shoulder. If you really need it to cook all day, it can do that too. Ole!

Vegetable oil spray

2 boneless skinless chicken thighs, cut in small bite-size pieces

3 cans (15 ounces or 425 g each) hominy, drained (yellow, white, or a combination)

1 medium onion, chopped fine

6 plump garlic cloves, minced

1 bay leaf

4 cups (940 ml) low-sodium chicken broth

1 jar or can (14 to 16 ounces, or 396 to 455 g) red enchilada sauce

Kosher salt or coarse sea salt

Shredded cabbage, radish slices, thin rings of fresh jalapeño, and lime wedges, for garnishes

① Generously spray the inside of the slow cooker with oil.

② In the slow cooker, combine the chicken, hominy, onion, garlic, bay leaf, broth, and enchilada sauce. Cover and cook for 2 to 2½ on the high heat setting, or 6 to 8 hours on low. Add salt, if needed. Discard the bay leaf.

③ Ladle posole into bowls, and offer garnishes to customize each portion.

MAHOGANY-STAINED TURKEY LEGS

Here's some faux Q, a home version of the fair favorite. It works best in an oval cooker.

Vegetable oil spray

Six 12-ounce (340 g) turkey drumsticks, skin removed

1 teaspoon kosher salt or coarse sea salt, or more to taste

1 teaspoon coarse-ground black pepper

1 cup (260 g) tomato-based barbecue sauce

½ cup (120 ml) strong coffee

2 teaspoons (5 g) chili powder unless the barbecue sauce used is very spicy

1. Generously spray the inside of the slow cooker with oil. Spray the drumsticks with oil and coat well with salt and pepper.

2. Place the turkey drumsticks in the slow cooker, laying them in criss-cross directions from opposite ends, as needed to fit them in. Add the barbecue sauce, coffee, and chili powder (if using). Cover and cook on the high heat setting for 5 to 5½ hours or low for 8½ to 9 hours.

3. Uncover and cook for about 30 minutes more for the saucy mixture to dry out just a bit. Serve hot.

TURKEY BREAST

YIELD: SERVES 6 | COOKING TIME: 4½ TO 5½ HOURS ON LOW, CAN BE HELD 1 HOUR ON WARM

Did you know there's a Turkey, Texas? It's more famous though for Bob Wills, the King of Western Swing, than for Thanksgiving birds. There is, however, one place in the state famous for turkey—Greenberg's in Tyler. Many a turkey that has graced our family table has flapped its way in from Greenberg's.

Vegetable oil spray

1 tablespoon (15 ml) garlic oil

1 tablespoon (15 ml) liquid from a jar of pickled jalapeños, or cider vinegar

2 teaspoons (10 g) smoked salt, such as Maldon, or kosher salt or coarse sea salt

1 teaspoon freshly ground black pepper

4½- to 5-pound (2.1- to 2.3-kg) boneless skinless turkey breast

① Generously spray the inside of the slow cooker with oil. With several lengths of kitchen twine, tie the turkey breast, more or less, into a neat rectangle.

② In a small bowl, combine the garlic oil, jalapeño liquid, salt, and pepper. Rub the mixture all over the turkey breast. Transfer the turkey to the slow cooker. Cover and cook on the low heat setting until an instant-read thermometer, inserted deep into the breast, registers 160°F (71°C).

③ Transfer the turkey to a cutting board. Tent the turkey with foil and let rest for 15 minutes. Slice thinly across the grain of the meat. Spoon any juices from the cooker over the turkey slices, and serve hot or cold.

TURKEY MOLE

YIELD: SERVES 6 OR MORE | COOKING TIME: 4 TO 4½ HOURS ON HIGH, 8 TO 9 HOURS ON LOW

Mexican mole, even when made in shortcut fashion, can develop lots of complexity from its lengthy time in a slow cooker. The shortcut here is to start out with a store-bought jarred version of black or red mole paste or a powdered mole mix. Find mole paste in the Mexican section of a well-stocked supermarket, or at a Mexican market, or from melissaguerra.com. If you have a favorite from-scratch version, it can be used here too.

Vegetable oil spray

4- to 4½-pound (1.8 to 2.1-kg) bone-in skinless turkey breast

Kosher salt or coarse sea salt

3 tablespoons (45 ml) olive oil

1 large onion, minced

About ½ cup (130 g) black or red mole paste

1 can (14 to 15 ounces, or 425 g) tomatoes, undrained

1 cup (235 ml) low-sodium chicken broth

Sesame seeds, for garnish

① Generously spray the inside of the slow cooker with oil. Spray the turkey breast all over, too. Rub the turkey breast with salt, between 1 and 2 teaspoons, then place it in the slow cooker.

② Make the mole sauce. Warm the olive oil in a medium skillet over medium heat. Add the onion and cook for about 5 minutes, until translucent. Mix in the mole paste, the tomatoes and juice, and the broth. Add salt, if needed, to the sauce. Pour the sauce over the turkey. Cover and cook on the high heat setting for 4 to 4½ hours or on low for 8 to 9 hours.

③ Transfer the turkey breast to a cutting board. A pair of tongs and a large sturdy spoon or fork will help with this process. Let the turkey breast sit for about 10 minutes, then slice across the grain. Spoon out mole sauce for each portion. Any leftovers of either turkey or sauce can be refrigerated together. If you wish, shred the turkey and mix it together with the sauce as a filling for enchiladas or other dishes.

SMOTHERED QUAIL

YIELD: SERVES 4 | COOKING TIME: 2½ TO 3 HOURS ON LOW, CAN BE HELD 1 HOUR ON WARM

Whether your quail are farm-raised or hunted, the classic Texas preparation calls for burying them in savory gravy. White rice is a good vehicle for soaking up the sauce.

Vegetable oil spray

8 quail, whole or split, about 6 ounces (168 g) each

Kosher salt or coarse sea salt

Freshly ground black pepper

4 slices thick-cut bacon, chopped fine

1 medium onion, chopped

4 garlic cloves, minced

3 celery stalks, chopped

3 ounces (85 g) button mushrooms, sliced thin

2 teaspoons (5 g) ground cumin

2 tablespoons (16 g) unbleached all-purpose flour

2 cups (470 ml) low-sodium chicken broth

1 tablespoon (15 g) Worcestershire sauce

① Generously spray the inside of the slow cooker with oil.

② Season the quail with salt and pepper and arrange them in the slow cooker, placing them over each other as needed in crisscross directions.

③ Fry the bacon in a medium skillet over medium heat. When brown and crisp, remove the bacon with a slotted spoon and reserve it on a paper towel. To the pan drippings, add the onion, garlic, celery, and mushrooms. Cover, reduce the heat to medium-low and sweat the mixture for 5 minutes. Uncover and add the cumin and flour. Stir and cook for 2 to 3 minutes, until fragrant. Pour about ½ cup (120 ml) of the broth into the skillet and scrape up from the bottom, loosening all of the browned bits. Scrape the mixture into the slow cooker. Pour the rest of the broth and the Worcestershire sauce over and cover.

④ Cook the quail for 2½ to 3 hours on low, until the quail are tender and cooked through. Scatter the bacon over the quail and serve 2 per person with some of the sauce.

6

GULF SEAFOOD AND FRESHWATER FISH

TEXAS MAY BE BEST KNOWN FOR BEEF, BUT IT SHOULD GET AS MUCH RECOGNITION FOR ITS PRODUCTION OF SHELLFISH, SUCH AS SHRIMP, OYSTERS, AND BLUE CRAB, AND FINFISH, SUCH AS SNAPPER, REDFISH, AND BLACK DRUM.

BAY BOIL

YIELD: SERVES 6 | COOKING TIME: 2½ TO 3 HOURS ON HIGH, CAN BE HELD 1 HOUR ON WARM

Texas has some 365 miles of coastline on the Gulf of Mexico. The tourism folks refer to the coastline as the Coastal Bend. The state may be best known for beef, but it should get as much recognition for its production of shrimp, oysters, blue crab, and fish such as snapper, redfish, and black drum. I turned to *The Houston Junior League Cookbook* of 1968 when I came to the state in the 1970s and needed instructions for my first Texas seafood boil. The book was something of a standard setter in the gilded age of cookbooks from women's service organizations. The recipe of Mrs. Owen Finch inspired the version I have done ever since. It was some years later, though, that I tried it in the slow cooker and discovered that cooking it at the speed of a Houston rush hour works especially well. The shrimp and corn get a chance to absorb more robust flavor from the liquid than is typical in higher heat cooking.

Vegetable oil spray

1 large onion, sliced and pulled into rings

1 tablespoon dill seed

4 bay leaves

2 teaspoons (6 g) kosher salt or coarse sea salt

1 teaspoon black peppercorns

24 ounces (940 ml) beer, preferably a Mexican lager, such as Bohemia

1 large lemon, halved

3 pounds (1.4 kg) large shrimp in shells

3 ears fresh corn, cut in half

SAUCE

½ pound (2 sticks, or 225 g) unsalted butter

Juice of ½ lemon

1 teaspoon Worcestershire sauce

Few dashes Tabasco sauce

1. Generously spray the inside of the slow cooker with oil.

2. Combine in the slow cooker the onion, dill seed, bay leaves, salt, peppercorns, and beer. Squeeze in the lemon juice and then toss in both lemon shells. Cover and cook on high heat for 2 to 2½ hours. You are essentially infusing the beer with the flavors of the other ingredients.

3. Add the shrimp and corn to the boil, cover again, and continue cooking on high for about 30 minutes more, until the shrimp have turned translucent pink and corn is just tender.

4. While the shrimp and corn are cooking, make the sauce. Melt the butter over medium-low heat and stir in the lemon juice, Worcestershire sauce, and Tabasco sauce. Remove from the heat but keep warm.

5. With a slotted spoon, remove the shrimp and the corn, and some of the onion from the slow cooker and transfer it to a platter. Serve with the sauce for everyone to peel their own shrimp and dunk them in sauce, as they wish.

JAMBALAYA

YIELD: SERVES 6 | COOKING TIME: 3½ TO 4 HOURS ON HIGH

Of all the savory recipes in this book, jambalaya might be my personal favorite in almost every mood.

2 tablespoons (30 ml) vegetable oil (divided)

2 tablespoons (28 g) unsalted butter

4-ounce (115-g) link uncooked andouille sausage or other spicy sausage, sliced thin

2 cups (320 g) chopped onion

1 medium green bell pepper, chopped

1 cup (100 g) chopped celery

1 fresh jalapeño, minced

3 garlic cloves, minced

1 cup (185 g) long-grain rice, such as Texmati

2 teaspoons (3 g) dried thyme

2 bay leaves

¼ teaspoon ground cayenne, or more to taste

6 ounces (168 g) smoky ham, diced

1 teaspoon kosher salt or coarse sea salt, or more to taste

2 cups (470 ml) low-sodium seafood broth or chicken broth

18 medium shrimp, peeled (tails left on, if you wish) or ¾ pound (340 g) crawfish

① Grease the inside of the slow cooker with about 1 teaspoon of the oil.

② Warm the rest of the oil and the butter in a heavy large skillet over medium heat. Add andouille and cook for about 2 minutes, just long enough for it to begin to color. Stir in the onion, bell pepper, celery, jalapeño, and garlic, and sauté until the vegetables are tender, about 10 minutes. Add the rice, thyme, bay leaves, and cayenne, stir and cook for another minute. Spoon the mixture into the slow cooker.

③ Add the ham, salt, and broth to the slow cooker. Cover and cook on the high heat setting for 3 to 3½ hours, until rice is tender. Scatter the shrimp over the mixture, cover again, and cook until the shrimp are opaque and cooked through, about 30 more minutes. Add more salt, if needed. Remove the bay leaves. Spoon onto plates and serve.

SNAPPER-AND-SHELLFISH STEW

YIELD: SERVES 6 | COOKING TIME: 4½ TO 5½ HOURS ON LOW, ABOUT 3 TO 3½ HOURS ON HIGH

Something of a fisherman's stew, you can combine whatever fish and seafood happens to be freshest for this, as long as the quantities add up to something close to what is proposed here. Don't be afraid to try by-catch fish, sometimes less attractively referred to as "trash" fish, if recommended by your fishmonger.

1 tablespoon (15 ml) olive oil (divided)

4 ounces (115 g) bulk Mexican-style chorizo

1½ cups (240 g) chopped onion

8 plump garlic cloves, minced

12 ounces (340 g) russet potatoes, peeled and cut in ½-inch (1-cm) cubes

1 can (14 to 15 ounces, or 425 g) crushed tomatoes with puree

1 cup (235 ml) dry red wine, such as cabernet sauvignon

1 cup (235 ml) low-sodium seafood broth or 8-ounce bottle clam juice

1 teaspoon kosher salt or coarse sea salt, or more to taste

½ teaspoon freshly ground black pepper, or more to taste

1 pound (455 g) red snapper fillets, cut in 2-inch (5-cm) pieces

8 ounces (225 g) medium shrimp, peeled (tails left on if you wish)

8 ounces (225 g) blue crabmeat

½ cup (45 g) minced flat-leaf parsley

① Grease the inside of the slow cooker with about 1 teaspoon of the oil.

② Pour the rest of the oil into a medium skillet and warm it over medium-high heat. Add the chorizo. Cook until richly colored, breaking up the chorizo into very small pieces with a spatula. Add the onion and garlic to the skillet and cook for about 5 minutes, until starting to soften. Scrape into the slow cooker. Stir in the potatoes, tomatoes, wine, broth, salt, and pepper. Cover and cook for 4 to 5 hours on the low heat setting or 2½ to 3 hours on high, until the potatoes are very tender and the ingredients have melded together.

③ Add to the slow cooker the snapper, shrimp, and crab. Cover again and continue cooking for approximately 30 more minutes. The stew is ready when the snapper is flaky and shrimp are cooked through. Add more salt and pepper, if you wish. Stir in parsley. Ladle into bowls and serve.

GULF GUMBO

YIELD: SERVES 8 | COOKING TIME: 3½ TO 4 HOURS ON HIGH, CAN BE HELD ON WARM FOR AN HOUR

A gumbo is a call to celebrate. It might seem counter-intuitive to make dishes with quick-cooking ingredients, such as shrimp and oysters, in a slow cooker. However, the initial cooking of the recipe's "base" allows complexity to develop, and the gentle heat cooks the seafood through without toughening it or drying it out. A good gumbo always must start with a good roux, which I typically slow cook a day or two before making the gumbo itself. In the slow cooker, there's no worry about standing over the hot oil mixture for forty-five minutes, or of the roux burning and requiring a new start. Serve over steaming white rice in big bowls. For a party, accompany with a half-dozen bottles of Texas and Louisiana hot sauces.

Vegetable oil spray

½ cup Slow Roux (below)

4-ounce (115-g) link andouille sausage, sliced thin

2 medium onions, chopped

2 medium green bell peppers, chopped

3 medium celery stalks, chopped

5 garlic cloves, minced

1 bottle (8 ounce, or 235 ml) clam juice

3 cups (705 ml) low-sodium chicken broth

2 bay leaves

½ teaspoon ground cayenne pepper

½ teaspoon freshly ground black pepper

½ teaspoon ground dried thyme

¾ pound (340 g) peeled raw medium shrimp, tails off

½ to ¾ pound (225 to 340 g) lump blue crabmeat

10 to 12 shucked oysters, with their liquor

2 teaspoons (6 g) kosher salt or coarse sea salt, or more to taste

6 to 8 scallions, light green and white portions, sliced thin

1 tablespoon filé powder

Cooked white rice

✕ SLOW ROUX ✕

Stir together in the bottom of a slow cooker (whatever your smallest size) ¼ cup (59 ml) vegetable oil and ¼ cup (32 g) flour. Cook on the high heat setting for 8 to 10 hours, until the roux is richly deeply brown. Pour into a heatproof jar, let cool, and cover. Leave at room temperature if using within a day. Otherwise refrigerate. Roux will keep for several weeks.

① Generously spray the inside of the slow cooker with oil.

② Pour the roux into a medium skillet. Warm over medium heat and add to it the andouille, onions, bell peppers, celery, and garlic. Cook for 8 to 10 minutes until the vegetables are fairly tender. You don't want them to brown so turn down the heat a bit if needed. Pour in the clam juice and scrape up from the bottom to loosen all browned bits.

③ Scrape the mixture into the slow cooker. Add to it the chicken broth, bay leaves, cayenne, black pepper, and thyme. Cover and cook for 3 to 3½ hours on high. Stir in the shrimp, crabmeat, oysters, salt, scallions, and filé powder. Stir well. Cover again and cook for about 30 more minutes, until the shrimp and oysters are cooked through.

④ Serve the gumbo hot as blazes over rice.

FILÉ POWDER IS
MADE FROM GROUND
SASSAFRAS LEAVES,
THE THICKENING
AND FLAVORING
PROPERTIES OF
WHICH WERE FIRST
DISCOVERED BY THE
CHOCTAW PEOPLE.

GARLIC SHRIMP WITH VERMICELLI

YIELD: SERVES 6 | **COOKING TIME:** ABOUT 1½ HOURS ON HIGH

Texas coastal towns have struggled with issues affecting the shrimp and seafood industry, from cheap cut-rate imports to expensive fuel and ecological concerns. Palacios, equidistant from Galveston and Corpus Christi, endures though as the self-described Shrimp Capital of Texas. In honor of the number of Vietnamese families who settled the area in decades past, this version of shrimp includes some familiar Vietnamese flavors. The slow, sealed cooking allows the shrimp to absorb fully the flavor of the garlic and remain very tender.

¼ cup (59 ml) vegetable oil

12 plump garlic cloves, sliced thin

1 tablespoon chopped lemongrass

1 cup (140 g) vermicelli, broken into
 1- to 2-inch (2.5- to 5-cm) pieces

2 pounds (905 g) peeled uncooked
 large shrimp, with or without tails

2 tablespoons (32 g) Asian fish sauce

1 tablespoon (15 ml) rice vinegar
 or white vinegar

½ cup (48 g) fresh mint, chopped

½ cup (24 g) fresh basil, chopped

① Combine the oil, garlic, and lemongrass in the slow cooker, cover, and cook for about 30 minutes until fragrant.

② Stir in the vermicelli, shrimp, fish sauce, and vinegar. Cover again and cook for 45 to 60 minutes more, until the shrimp and vermicelli are both cooked through and tender. Transfer the shrimp mixture to a platter, scatter mint and basil over it, and serve.

BLUE CRAB AND RICE GRATIN

YIELD: SERVES 6 | COOKING TIME: 2 TO 2½ HOURS ON LOW

Rice grows in southeast Texas not far from the coast, where blue crabs abound. They mix it up here in casserole form with artichoke hearts. Artichokes are not exactly a major local crop but they do have a long history of popularity in Texas cookbooks. After slow cooking, the gratin gets a topper of crunchy bread crumbs.

Vegetable oil spray

1 pound (455 g) lump blue crabmeat

2 cups (316 g) cooked white or brown rice

½ cup (75 g) finely chopped red bell pepper

1 fresh jalapeño or serrano chile, minced

Zest and juice of 1 lemon

1½ tablespoons (21 g) Worcestershire sauce

Kosher salt or coarse sea salt

8 ounces (225 g) cream cheese, cut in ½-inch (1-cm) cubes

1 tablespoon (14 g) unsalted butter

1 cup (120 g) dried bread crumbs

① Generously spray the inside of the slow cooker with oil.

② Combine in the slow cooker the crab, rice, bell pepper, jalapeño, lemon zest and juice, Worcestershire sauce, and salt to taste. Stir the mixture together. Dot the top with the cream cheese cubes. Cover and cook on the low heat setting for 2 to 2½ hours until hot and nicely melded together.

③ In a small skillet, warm the butter over medium heat. Stir in the bread crumbs and cook until fragrant and crunchy. Scatter the bread crumbs over the crab dish. Spoon out and serve hot.

REDFISH, GROUPER, SNAPPER, OR LAKE BASS WITH EASY BARBECUE REMOULADE

YIELD: SERVES 6 | COOKING TIME: 1 HOUR ON LOW

Remoulade sauce, a timeless pairing with seafood, is something of a fancied-up tartar sauce. In this case, it gets a little added oomph from barbecue sauce.

Vegetable oil spray

6 fillets redfish, grouper, snapper, or lake bass, about 6 ounces (168 g) each

1 teaspoon sweet paprika

1 teaspoon kosher salt or coarse sea salt

1 medium lemon, halved

EASY BARBECUE REMOULADE SAUCE

½ cup (115 g) mayonnaise

¼ cup (84 g) whole-grain mustard

2 tablespoons (30 g) tomato-based barbecue sauce, such as Stubb's

1 tablespoon (15 ml) extra-virgin olive oil

3 cornichon pickles, minced, or 2 tablespoons (30 g) minced dill pickle

1 scallion, green and white portions, minced

① Generously spray the inside of the slow cooker with oil. Then spray the fish fillets with oil.

② Sprinkle the fish fillets with the paprika and salt. Arrange the fillets in the slow cooker. Squeeze the lemon juice over and around. Cover and cook for about 1 hour on the low heat setting, until the fillets are cooked through and flaky.

③ While the fish fillets are cooking, prepare the remoulade sauce. In a bowl, stir together the ingredients and refrigerate until needed.

④ Carefully scoop out the fish fillets with a fish spatula, and arrange on plates. Top with spoonfuls of remoulade sauce, and serve.

LAKE BASS WITH ORANGES AND ALMONDS

YIELD: SERVES 6 | COOKING TIME: 1 TO 2 HOURS ON HIGH

Texas has more square miles of inland water than even Minnesota and Florida. Anglers enthuse about the state's large-mouth bass fishing, in particular. Great opportunities abound, from Caddo Lake in the far northeast corner to Falcon and Amistad fed by the Rio Grande on the state's southern *frontera*. You can use other firm white fish fillets for this if you are fresh out of bass.

Vegetable oil spray

Six 6-ounce (168 g) lake bass fillets or other firm white fish fillets

Kosher salt or coarse sea salt

Freshly ground black pepper

Zest of 1 medium orange and juice of 2 medium oranges, about ⅔ cup

Juice of 1 medium lemon

2 teaspoons (14 g) Creole or brown mustard

2 tablespoons (15 g) slivered almonds

1 large orange, cut into 6 wedges, for garnish

① Generously spray the inside of the slow cooker with oil. Spray the bass fillets on both sides with oil, then sprinkle them with salt and pepper.

② In a small bowl, use a fork to whisk together the orange zest and juice, lemon juice, and mustard.

③ Lay fish fillets flat in the bottom of the slow cooker. When you have 1 layer, pour half of the orange juice mixture over them. Layer the remaining fillets over and pour on the rest of the orange juice mixture. Cover and cook on the high heat setting for 1 to 2 hours, until the fillets are all cooked through and flaky.

④ Scoop the fillets out onto plates or a platter. Garnish each portion with an orange wedge, sprinkle with almonds, and serve right away.

SNAPPER VERCRUZ, PROBABLY THE MOST POPULAR FISH DISH IN MEXICO, IS TOO OFTEN DRENCHED IN A PASTY TOMATO SAUCE. IF THAT IS THE ONLY WAY YOU HAVE HAD IT, THIS VERSION, MADE WITH FRESH TOMATOES, WILL BE A HAPPY REVELATION.

SNAPPER VERACRUZ

YIELD: SERVES 4 | COOKING TIME: 3 TO 4 HOURS ON LOW

One of the signatures of Gulf cooking, this famous fish preparation comes from farther down the coast, from Veracruz, one of Mexico's largest and oldest port cities. The dish tastily represents the melding of the New World tomato with many of the ingredients that were brought here from Spain, including olives, olive oil, garlic, capers, parsley, bay leaves, cinnamon, and black pepper.

SAUCE

2 tablespoons (20 ml) olive oil (divided)

1 medium onion, chopped

4 garlic cloves, minced

½ teaspoon crumbled dried Mexican oregano or dried marjoram

¼ teaspoon ground cinnamon

1 pound (455 g) red-ripe fresh tomatoes, chopped, or 2 cups (360 g) canned crushed tomatoes

¼ cup low-sodium seafood broth or chicken broth

¼ cup (15 g) flat-leaf parsley (divided)

½ cup sliced pimiento-stuffed green olives

1 pickled jalapeño, seeded and minced, plus 1 teaspoon jalapeño pickling liquid

1 tablespoon (8 g) small capers

2 bay leaves

1½ teaspoons Worcestershire sauce

1 teaspoon kosher salt or coarse sea salt

½ teaspoon coarse-ground black pepper

SNAPPER

Four 6-ounce (168 g) red snapper fillets or other firm-fleshed but flaky white fish fillets

Juice of 2 medium limes

Kosher salt or coarse sea salt

Zest and juice of 1 medium lime

① Grease the inside of the slow cooker with about 1 teaspoon of the oil.

② Warm the remaining oil in a skillet over medium heat. Stir in the onion and garlic, and cook until the onion is limp and translucent, about 5 minutes. Stir in the oregano and cinnamon, and cook for about 1 more minute, until fragrant. Remove from the heat and scrape into the slow cooker.

③ Add to the slow cooker the tomatoes, broth, one-half of the parsley, olives, jalapeños and pickling liquid, capers, bay leaves, Worcestershire sauce, salt, and pepper. Stir, cover, and cook for 2 to 3 hours on low, until vegetables are all tender and the mixture has melded into a sauce.

④ About 30 minutes before you expect the sauce to be ready, lay the snapper fillets in a shallow dish. Squeeze lime juice over them and turn them over once in the juice. Sprinkle with salt. Let the fillets sit in the juice at room temperature. If the sauce takes more than 30 minutes to cook, drain the lime juice from the fillets and refrigerate them until needed.

⑤ Transfer the fillets to the slow cooker. Push each fillet down into the sauce to mostly cover it. Scatter with lime zest and squeeze on the lime juice. Cover and continue cooking for about 1 more hour on low, until the snapper is cooked through and flaky. Scoop the fillets up carefully, and arrange on plates or a platter. Pool some of the sauce over and around each fillet. Scatter with remaining parsley and serve.

7

BEANS, VEGETABLES, AND OTHER SIDES

A STELLAR POT OF DRUNKEN PINTOS

YIELD: SERVES 6 TO 8 | COOKING TIME: 10 TO 11 HOURS ON LOW, 5 TO 6 HOURS ON HIGH, CAN BE HELD ON WARM FOR SEVERAL HOURS

When I arrived in Texas in the 1970s, I had a bean epiphany. Apparently, I had never been fed anything other than canned beans until that point in my life, and I was quite adamant about my dislike for those. I made such a stink about how much I reviled canned beans that they became the source of a running family joke. I was given a can of beans every Christmas by my parents, hidden inside of other gifts, until my mother passed away in 2015. Neither she nor my dad drank alcohol, so this pot of beans would have been lost on them. Cooking beans low and slow in the slow cooker is close to the way beans are cooked traditionally in bean pots over smoldering fires. They come out super creamy and bursting with goodness. With cornbread, a bowl of these beans makes a classic comfort supper.

Vegetable oil spray

1 pound (455 g) dried pinto beans, picked over and rinsed

½ medium onion, minced

1 or 2 fresh or pickled jalapeños, sliced thin

4 whole thick-cut bacon slices

3 cups (705 ml) water

1 bottle or can (12 ounces, or 355 ml) medium-bodied beer

1 teaspoon kosher salt or coarse sea salt, or more to taste

1 teaspoon coarsely ground black pepper

① Generously spray the inside of the slow cooker with oil.

② Stir together the beans, onion, jalapeños, bacon, water, and beer in the slow cooker. Cover and cook until the beans are quite tender, 10 to 11 hours on the low heat setting or 5 to 6 hours on high.

③ Stir salt and pepper into beans and, if the mixture is thick, a bit more water, too. The beans should be a bit soupy. Spoon out and serve. Leftovers are good for a couple of days and make a great filling, drained of liquid, for tacos, burritos, and more.

BAKED BEANS

YIELD: SERVES 6 OR MORE | COOKING TIME: 10 TO 11 HOURS ON LOW, 5 TO 6 HOURS ON HIGH, CAN BE HELD ON WARM FOR SEVERAL HOURS

Sportsman and frontier novelist Hart Stilwell, from Brownsville, often bragged about his abilities to cook beans. This recipe allegedly began with him, and I am guessing would have included initially, perhaps, the coffee, molasses, and maybe the bourbon, too. Marie Riha, a contemporary of his from South Texas, passed on her "housebroken" version of the beans to her daughter, a friend of mine. I think the two ladies probably adjusted Stilwell's recipe a good bit, because it's difficult for me to imagine him out on the range with a carrot, among other details. One thing I know for sure is that the beans are darned good, the reason I adapted them myself to the slow cooker. If you're not a fan of bourbon, simply leave it out.

Vegetable oil spray

1 pound (455 g) dried navy beans, picked over and rinsed

½ medium red onion, chopped

1 medium carrot, grated fine

2 thick-cut bacon slices, chopped fine

2 tablespoons molasses or sorghum molasses

2 tablespoons (30 g) packed brown sugar

2 tablespoons (30 g) tomato-based barbecue sauce, such as Stubb's

2 tablespoons (42 g) brown mustard

4 cups (940 ml) water, or more as needed

1 can (8 ounces, or 225 g) tomato sauce

¾ cup (175 ml) strong brewed coffee

¼ cup (60 ml) bourbon or additional water

1 teaspoon kosher salt or coarse sea salt, or more to taste

① Generously spray the inside of the slow cooker with oil.

② Stir together the beans, onion, carrot, bacon, molasses, brown sugar, barbecue sauce, mustard, water, tomato sauce, coffee, and bourbon in the slow cooker. Cover and cook until the beans are quite tender, 10 to 11 hours on the low heat setting or 5 to 6 hours on high. Toward the end of the cooking time, make sure there's enough liquid to at least stay even with the level of beans in the pot. Salt can be added in the last hour or so of cooking time.

③ Spoon out and serve.

BLACK-EYED PEAS WITH HAM HOCKS

YIELD: SERVES 6 | COOKING TIME: 5½ TO 6 HOURS ON HIGH, 11 TO 12 HOURS ON LOW, CAN BE HELD ON WARM FOR SEVERAL HOURS

Black-eyed peas were new to me when I moved to Texas in the mid-1970s. I soon learned to love them, as prepared by the mother of a friend. One of the things I know I liked about her flavoring of them was the use of Spice Islands Beau Monde seasoning. That was something else I had never heard of, even though it had been around since the 1940s. She used it to flavor many things, so much so that I came to think of this blend—essentially of celery salt and onion salt—as THE Texas seasoning. If you have Spice Islands Beau Monde, by all means use 2 teaspoons (6 g) of it here in place of the suggested celery salt and onion salt.

1 pound (455 g) dried black-eyed peas

4 cups (940 ml) water, or more as needed

1-pound (455-g) smoked ham hock, cut in several pieces by your butcher

1 medium onion, chopped

2 garlic cloves, minced

2 bay leaves

1 medium green bell pepper, chopped

2 tablespoons (30 ml) white vinegar or cider vinegar

1 teaspoon freshly ground black pepper

1 teaspoon celery salt

1 teaspoon onion salt

① Combine everything in the slow cooker.

② Cover and cook on the high heat setting for 5½ to 6 hours or on low for 11 to 12 hours, until the black-eyed peas are very tender. Discard the bay leaves. Serve hot with some of the "pot likker."

BLACK-EYED PEAS AND COLLARDS

YIELD: SERVES 6 | COOKING TIME: 6 HOURS ON HIGH, 11 TO 12 HOURS ON LOW, CAN BE HELD ON WARM FOR SEVERAL HOURS

Don't restrict the symbol of good luck to just one day. A soothing bowl of peas and collards is perfect for New Year's Day or just about any other day of the year. I like these best when the collards cook for about half the time of the dried peas. However, if you want to make this and will not be at home to add the collards later, simply toss it all together at the start. It will still be good.

1 pound (455 g) dried black-eyed peas

4 thick-cut bacon slices

3 celery stalks, chopped

5 plump garlic cloves, minced

2 bay leaves

½ teaspoon dried thyme

½ teaspoon kosher salt or coarse
    sea salt

4 cups (940 ml) chicken broth,
    preferably low-sodium

1 cup (235 ml) water

½ teaspoon Tabasco sauce

¾ pound (340 g) roughly chopped
    collard greens

① Combine everything but the collard greens in the slow cooker.

② Cover and cook on the high heat setting for about 3 hours. Add the collards to the top of the slow cooker, cover again quickly, and cook for approximately 3 more hours. You may add the collards in the middle of the cooking time on low heat, if you wish. The dish is ready when both the black-eyed peas and collard greens are very tender. Discard the bay leaves. Serve hot with some of the "pot likker."

RED BEANS AND RICE

YIELD: SERVES 6 OR MORE | COOKING TIME: 10 TO 11 HOURS ON LOW, 5 TO 6 HOURS ON HIGH, CAN BE HELD ON WARM FOR SEVERAL HOURS

Red beans and rice, rightly, is an iconic dish of New Orleans—but good things don't necessarily stay within state borders. Louisiana's Cajuns, in particular, moved westward to Texas in both the nineteenth and twentieth centuries for work in oil fields, shipyards, and construction. Of course, *étouffée* and other dishes like this came along with them, and then spread. I found the addition of a jalapeño in the 1976 *A Texas Hill Country Cookbook*. Red beans and red kidney beans are not the same, but it's okay to use the slightly larger kidney beans more common outside of Creole and Cajun country. The beans are best with an overnight of soaking before cooking, so plan accordingly. Again, low, slow heat results in silky beans.

1 pound (455 g) dried red beans
    or red kidney beans

Vegetable oil spray

1½ pounds (680 g) ham hocks,
    in pieces

2 medium onions, chopped fine

1 large green bell pepper, chopped fine

¾ cup (75 g) chopped celery

4 garlic cloves, minced

1 fresh or pickled jalapeño, minced

2 bay leaves

1 teaspoon dried thyme

2 teaspoons (6 g) kosher salt or coarse
    sea salt, or more to taste

Cooked white rice

Hot sauce, such as Tabasco or Crystal

1. The night before you plan to cook the beans, cover them with water to twice the height of the beans and let them sit overnight.

2. Generously spray the inside of the slow cooker with oil.

3. Dump the beans and their soaking liquid into the slow cooker. Add the ham hocks, onions, bell pepper, celery, garlic, jalapeño, bay leaves, and thyme, and then add more water as needed to cover the whole bean mixture. Cover and cook for 10 to 11 hours on the low heat setting, or 5 to 6 on high. Beans are ready when very tender. Uncover and add salt to the beans. Remove about one-half cup of the beans and their liquid and mash well. Stir mashed beans back into the cooker. Cover and continue cooking about 15 minutes more.

4. Spoon rice into large bowls. Spoon red beans over the rice, and serve accompanied by hot sauce.

BAKED POTATOES THAT CAN BE DRESSED TO KILL

YIELD: SERVES 4 TO 8 | COOKING TIME: PRETTY MUCH ALL DAY ON LOW (8 TO 11 HOURS)

A college friend of mine was completely enamored of cooking baked potatoes in the microwave, back when the microwave was still a new and novel appliance. Yes, back when dinosaurs roamed the Earth. I never thought the texture of those nuked potatoes was notable. I do think you can take the opposite approach, slowing the cooking down, and end up with a very tender "baked" potato, one that can be quickly dressed in traditional finery of butter, salt, sour cream, and more, or stuffed with those goodies plus cheese and returned to the heat to make a twice-baked spud.

4 to 8 12-ounce (340 g) russet potatoes

① If you plan to rescue the potatoes within 8 hours or so, rub them with vegetable oil and toss them in the slow cooker. If the time is more likely to be 10 to 11 hours, wrap each in foil, to avoid the skin getting tough.

② Toss them in the slow cooker and cover that sucker. Come back to your nice hot potatoes some hours later. Enjoy.

MAC & CHEESE WITH A TEXAS TWIST

YIELD: SERVES 4 TO 6 AS A MAIN DISH, 6 TO 8 AS A SIDE DISH | COOKING TIME: 3 TO 3½ HOURS ON LOW

Yes, you can simply stir together raw macaroni with other common ingredients and let it gently, deliberately morph into a finished dish. Mac & cheese might be a side dish in an East Texas café or at a backyard barbecue, and of course, it can make a worthy main dish, too. Here it's zipped up with a little locally favored pizzazz. Canned Ro-Tel brand tomatoes and green chiles are as common in supermarkets as Lone Star beer.

MAC & CHEESE

Vegetable oil spray

1 pound (455 g) uncooked elbow macaroni

4 cups (480 g) shredded medium Cheddar cheese (divided)

2 cans (12 ounces or 355 ml each) evaporated milk

2 cups (470 ml) whole or 2% milk, or 1 cup (235 ml) whole milk and 1 cup (235 ml) buttermilk

1 can (10 ounces, or 280 g) tomatoes and green chiles, such as Ro-Tel

1 teaspoon kosher salt or coarse sea salt

1 teaspoon dry mustard or Dijon mustard

BREAD CRUMBS

1 tablespoon (14 g) unsalted butter

¾ cup (38 g) dried bread crumbs, preferably panko crumbs

① Generously spray the inside of the slow cooker with oil.

② Combine in the slow cooker the macaroni, 3 generous cups (380 g) cheese, evaporated milk, whole milk, tomatoes and green chiles, salt, and mustard. Stir together pushing the macaroni down into the liquid.

③ Cover and cook on low for about 2½ hours. It will look soupy and unpromising for most of the cooking time.

④ Prepare the bread crumbs while the macaroni and cheese is cooking. First melt the butter in a small skillet over medium heat. Stir in the bread crumbs and toast them until golden brown, stirring occasionally. Scrape the bread crumbs out of the skillet and reserve them.

⑤ Check the progress of the macaroni and cheese. If it appears to be setting up, stir once well, top with remaining cheese and toasted bread crumbs. If it is still not ready, check again after approximately 30 more minutes.

⑥ Cover only partially with the lid and cook for 20 to 30 more minutes, until cheese on top has melted and bread crumbs are crunchy.

MAC & CHEESE MIGHT BE A SIDE DISH IN AN EAST TEXAS CAFÉ OR AT A BACKYARD BARBECUE, BUT IT CAN MAKE A WORTHY MAIN DISH, TOO.

SIMPLE SCALLOPED POTATOES

YIELD: SERVES 6 TO 8 | COOKING TIME: 5 TO 6 HOURS ON LOW

Not cheesed or jalapeñoed or otherwise floofed up—these potatoes offer just elemental creamy goodness. It's dead easy to put these together, especially if you have a mandoline to slice the potatoes.

3 tablespoons (42 g) unsalted butter, cut in about 18 bits (divided)

2 cups (470 ml) half-and-half

3 pounds (1.4 kg) russet potatoes (about 5 medium), peeled and sliced ¼ inch (6 mm) thick

2 teaspoons (6 g) unbleached all-purpose flour

1½ teaspoons kosher salt or coarse sea salt, or more to taste

½ teaspoon dried thyme, optional

Freshly ground black pepper

① Generously grease the inside of the slow cooker with about 1 teaspoon of the butter.

② Layer the ingredients in semi-organized fashion. Start with 1 to 2 tablespoons (15 to 30 ml) of half-and-half, enough just to cover the bottom of the cooker. Next add 2 layers of potatoes, shingled beside and slightly over each other. Pour on about one-third of the half-and-half. Dot with one-third of the remaining butter bits and just over ½ teaspoon of flour. Sprinkle with ½ teaspoon of salt, about one-third of the thyme, and a grinding of black pepper. Repeat with two more layers of potatoes and other ingredients.

③ Cover and cook on the low heat setting until potatoes are quite tender, 5 to 6 hours. Let the potatoes sit at room temperature for 15 minutes, then spoon out and serve.

SWEET POTATO GRATIN

YIELD: SERVES 6 OR MORE | COOKING TIME: 4 TO 5 HOURS ON LOW, CAN BE HELD ON WARM FOR 2 HOURS

Precooked sweet potatoes can go into a slow cooker with gobs of sugar and marshmallows and more, but I have never been a fan. I far prefer them with just a little sweetening so it's possible to really enjoy their natural flavor.

1 tablespoon (14 g) unsalted butter

2 pounds (905 g) sweet potatoes, peeled and grated

1 tangy apple, such as Granny Smith, peeled and grated

1 tablespoon (25 g) turbinado sugar (divided)

1 teaspoon kosher salt or coarse sea salt

½ teaspoon crumbled dried sage

Freshly ground black pepper

1 cup (235 ml) heavy cream

Fresh sage leaves for garnish, optional

① Generously grease the inside of the slow cooker with butter. Leave excess butter in the bottom.

② In a mixing bowl, combine the sweet potatoes, apple, 2 teaspoons (9 g) of sugar, salt, sage, and several grinds of pepper. Pat mixture into the slow cooker. Pour the cream over it. Sprinkle the remaining 1 teaspoon of sugar over the top. Cover and cook for 4 to 5 hours on the low heat setting, until the sweet potatoes are very tender.

③ Spoon out portions and serve. Garnish, if you wish, with sage leaves.

I WAS NEVER TOO CRAZY ABOUT THE BIG HIT OF GRASSY GREEN FLAVOR YOU GET WHEN YOU USE GREEN BELL PEPPERS FOR STUFFING. I PREFER BELL PEPPERS OF WARMER TONES—YELLOW, ORANGE, AND RED—FOR THEIR SWEETER FLAVOR.

STUFFED BELL PEPPERS

YIELD: SERVES 4 | COOKING TIME: 4 TO 4½ HOURS ON HIGH

Green bell peppers used to be pretty much the norm for stuffing. I was never too crazy about the big hit of grassy green flavor. A lot of them have rather thin walls too, which makes them less than optimum for standing up straight and tall like good soldiers while baking. When ripe bell peppers of warmer tones—yellow, orange, and red—became more common, I began using them because their flavor is sweeter and, to me at least, more harmonious for eating in their entirety. I prefer the consistency of the rice when these are cooked on high. However, if your time is such that you need to leave them for most of the day, double the time and use your low setting. They will still be good. A handful of corn kernels or a chopped small—very small—zucchini would be a fine addition here, if you like.

4 large meaty bell peppers, preferably 2 yellow and 2 orange, or 4 of either

1 can (14 to 15 ounces, or 425 g) pinto beans, drained and rinsed, or 1¾ cups home-cooked pintos

1 can (10 ounces, or 280 g) mild-to-medium heat red enchilada sauce (divided)

½ cup (92 g) uncooked white rice

¼ cup (30 g) shredded mild Cheddar cheese

1 tablespoon (3 g) minced chives, plus more for garnish, or thin-sliced green tops of 2 or 3 scallions

1 garlic clove, minced

Kosher salt or coarse sea salt, to taste

¼ cup (56 g) crumbled queso fresco, or additional mild Cheddar cheese

① Generously spray the inside of the slow cooker with oil.

② Slice a thin layer off the bottom of the bell peppers, as needed for each to stand up. Neatly slice the top off each pepper, about ½ inch (1 cm) below the stem, then cut out and discard each pepper's seeds and ribs. Chop the tops of the peppers.

③ In a bowl, mix together the chopped pepper tops, beans, 1 cup of the enchilada sauce, rice, Cheddar cheese, chives, garlic, and a couple of good pinches of salt. The filling will be soupy because the extra liquid is needed to cook the rice. Spoon this filling into the peppers equally, just below the top of each. You need a little room for the rice to expand. Pour any remaining filling into the bottom of the cooker where it can meld into a sauce. Top each with queso fresco. If you are using additional Cheddar cheese, however, reserve it until the peppers are nearly done so that it doesn't dry out too much.

④ Arrange the peppers standing up in the slow cooker. Pour the remaining enchilada sauce around them. Cover and cook on the high heat setting for approximately 4 hours, until the rice and peppers are tender and juicy. If you are using Cheddar cheese as the topping, sprinkle it equally over the peppers after about 3½ hours, so that it has time to melt. Arrange peppers in shallow bowls or deep plates, with the juices spooned over them. Top with additional chives and serve.

JALAPEÑO JOMINY

YIELD: SERVES 6 | COOKING TIME: 3 TO 3½ HOURS ON LOW

Yes, it's really hominy. I'm just playing with you.

Vegetable oil spray

2 cans (15 ounces or 425 g each)
hominy, 1 white and 1 yellow,
if available, drained

2 tablespoons (28 g) unsalted butter

½ medium onion, chopped fine

½ red bell pepper, chopped fine

1 to 2 fresh jalapeños, chopped fine

2 tablespoons (28 ml) whole milk
or half-and-half

Kosher salt or coarse sea salt, optional

3 ounces (85 g) mild Cheddar cheese,
grated

3 ounces (85 g) Monterey Jack
or pepper Jack, grated

1. Generously spray the inside of the slow cooker with oil.

2. Pour the hominy into the slow cooker.

3. Warm the butter in a large skillet over medium heat. Sauté the onion and bell pepper about 5 minutes, until the onion is translucent. Spoon the mixture over the hominy. Add to it the jalapeño and milk. Cover and cook on the low heat setting for 2½ to 3 hours. Add salt if needed and scatter both cheeses over the hominy. Cook for an additional 30 minutes.

4. Serve hot.

CREAMY JALAPEÑO SPINACH

YIELD: SERVES 6 OR MORE | COOKING TIME: 3 TO 3½ HOURS ON LOW, WILL HOLD ON WARM FOR SEVERAL HOURS

Since the fortunate stumbling upon a jalapeño spinach recipe in a 1976 Dallas Junior League cookbook, a version of the dish has appeared on every holiday table in the extended Jamison and Alters families. It doesn't matter if it's Thanksgiving, Christmas, the 4th of July, or Texas Independence Day, you'll find it. The only thing that is argued these days is whether to use cream of mushroom soup or Cheez Whiz, both of which appeared in the original recipe. I come down on the side of ridding the recipe of both processed products, but I am sometimes overruled at family gatherings. What we can agree on is to top it with crushed French-fried onion rings, those ones from the can.

Unsalted butter

2 packages (10 ounces or 280 g each) frozen spinach, thawed and drained by squeezing spinach well

12 ounces (1½ cups) crème fraiche or Mexican crema

1 cup (4 ounces, or 115 g) grated Cheddar cheese

2 tablespoons (18 g) minced pickled jalapeños plus 1 or more tablespoons jalapeño pickling liquid

2 tablespoons (20 g) minced onion

2 tablespoons (15 g) minced celery

1 tablespoon (8 g) unbleached all-purpose flour

½ teaspoon kosher salt or coarse sea salt

Freshly ground black pepper

¾ to 1 cup (42 to 56 g) lightly crushed, canned, French-fried onion rings

① Generously grease the inside of the slow cooker with butter.

② Stir together in the slow cooker the spinach, crème fraiche, Cheddar, jalapeños, onion, celery, flour, salt, and a few good grinds of pepper. Smooth the top of the mixture. Cover and cook for 3 to 3½ hours on the low heat setting until the vegetables are very tender.

③ Scoop out about 1 cup of the spinach mixture and transfer to a blender. Zap a few times until very smooth. Mix back into the slow cooker.

④ Either top the spinach mixture in the slow cooker with the French-fried onions or sprinkle them over each portion. Eat right away.

CREOLE CABBAGE

YIELD: SERVES 6 OR MORE | COOKING TIME: 4½ TO 5 HOURS ON LOW, 2 TO 2½ HOURS ON HIGH

OKAY, okay, it doesn't sound very exciting. You may think, too, that cabbage as a side dish is tolerable just once a year, on St. Patrick's Day. Would it seem more thrilling if you knew that Kenneth Threadgill, the guy who gave Janis Joplin her real start, dished up a version of this in his converted gas station-café in Austin? If you're serving the cabbage at a potluck or other meal, where there may be more than six people sampling it, cut the cabbage in half-inch (1-cm) ribbons instead of wedges.

Vegetable oil spray

3 thick-cut bacon slices, chopped

1 large cabbage head (about 2 pounds, or 905 g), sliced in 6 wedges

1 medium onion, chopped

2 garlic cloves, minced

1 can (15 ounces, or 425 g) diced tomatoes with juice

1 tablespoon (16 g) tomato paste

1 teaspoon kosher salt or coarse sea salt, or more to taste

½ teaspoon freshly ground black pepper

½ cup (120 ml) low-sodium chicken broth

Several dashes red or green Tabasco sauce

1. Generously spray the inside of the slow cooker with oil.

2. Layer the ingredients in the slow cooker. Cover and cook on the low heat setting for 4½ to 5 hours or on high for 2 to 2½ hours, until the cabbage and onions are very tender.

3. Ladle cabbage wedges out with a slotted spoon. Then spoon some of the diced tomato, onion, and bacon from the bottom of the slow cooker over each portion, and serve.

GENNIE'S-STYLE ACORN SQUASH

YIELD: SERVES 6 OR 8 | COOKING TIME: 3½ TO 4 HOURS ON HIGH

"...the immortal grandmother of Dallas' home-cooking restaurants, everyone's home-away-from-home," exclaimed the *Dallas Observer* back in 1994. The paper was talking about Gennie's Bishop Grill, which required crossing the Trinity River to Oak Cliff. Back in the mid- and later 1970s, long before the area became celebrated as the Bishop Arts District, the idea of going south over the Houston Street bridge to eat raised a few eyebrows among north Dallas-ites. That never fazed me. I was always on the hunt for great food. Gennie's has been gone for some years now, but I still daydream about the vegetables with a Southern soul, and the cast-iron, skillet-cooked, chicken-fried steak of the café's heyday.

Vegetable oil spray

2 tablespoons (28 ml) water

2-pound (905-g) acorn squash

4 tablespoons (½ stick, or 55 g) unsalted butter, softened

2 tablespoons (30 g) packed brown sugar

1 teaspoon pure vanilla extract

¼ teaspoon kosher salt or coarse sea salt, or more to taste

¼ teaspoon ground cinnamon

⅛ teaspoon ground cloves

① Generously spray the inside of the slow cooker with oil. Pour in the water.

② Carefully cut the acorn squash in half. Remove and discard the seeds and fibers. Cut each squash half into 3 or 4 sections. Arrange the squash sections in the slow cooker, skin-side down. Try to get the squash sections into a single layer, but stack a piece or two, if needed.

③ Combine in a small bowl the butter, brown sugar, vanilla, salt, cinnamon, and cloves. Spoon the mixture evenly over the cut side of each piece of squash. Cover and cook on the high heat setting for 3½ to 4 hours until the squash is tender. When you open the slow cooker, spoon portions of the butter mixture back over the squash sections and serve.

THANKSGIVING DRESSING

YIELD: SERVES 6 OR MORE | COOKING TIME: ABOUT 3½ HOURS ON HIGH

You don't need to save this dressing for once a year. However, using the slow cooker for it on Thanksgiving frees up at least part of the oven for other dishes. How smart is that? If oven space is truly a factor, toast the bread a day or two in advance, so you can skip that step on a busy morning. The recipe calls for all white bread, but you can make this in the same way using half crumbled cornbread (by weight), if you like. In either case, though, make sure that the bread itself has very little or no sugar. You might be surprised at how many white breads are loaded with it, in some form. Dressing shouldn't taste like dessert. That's what pumpkin pie is for. Dressing made in a slow cooker has a fairly moist texture, like stuffing cooked in the bird. Uncovering it at the end of the cooking time can give it a drier consistency with a few chewy edges.

Vegetable oil spray

1-pound (455-g) loaf white bread, cut in ¾-inch (2-cm) cubes

6 tablespoons (84 g) unsalted butter

2 cups (320 g) chopped onion

2 cups (200 g) chopped celery

5 to 6 ounces (140 to 168 g) button mushrooms, sliced thin

2 teaspoons (about 2 g) crumbled dried sage

1½ teaspoons dried thyme

1 teaspoon kosher salt or coarse sea salt

½ teaspoon freshly ground black pepper

1 large egg

½ teaspoon baking powder

2 cups (470 ml) low-sodium chicken broth

① Preheat the oven to 325°F (170°C, or gas mark 3). Generously spray the inside of the slow cooker with oil.

② Toast the bread cubes on 2 rimmed baking sheets for about 25 minutes, stirring once or twice, until lightly brown and crisp. Dump them in the slow cooker.

③ Warm the butter in a large skillet over medium heat. Stir in the onion, celery, and mushrooms, and sauté until very soft, about 8 minutes. Stir in the sage, thyme, salt, and pepper, and then scrape the vegetable mixture into the slow cooker. Whisk together the egg and baking powder with about ½ cup (120 ml) of the broth, and pour over the vegetable mixture. Stir the dressing together, while adding the rest of the broth.

④ Cover and cook on the high heat setting for 3 to 3¼ hours, until it appears set. Uncover and continue cooking with the lid off for about 30 minutes. You want the surface of the dressing to dry out a bit but it will remain nicely moist. Spoon up and serve hot.

Note: You can make this with seasoned croutons, too, and save yourself a little time. I would still recommend sautéing plenty of onion, celery, and mushrooms to go in it, but improvise as you wish.

MAKING THIS DRESSING—WHICH HAS A FAIRLY MOIST TEXTURE, LIKE STUFFING COOKED IN THE BIRD—IN THE SLOW COOKER FREES UP THE OVEN FOR OTHER THANKSGIVING DISHES.

STEWED OKRA

YIELD: SERVES 6 | COOKING TIME: 4 HOURS ON LOW, CAN BE HELD ON WARM FOR 1 MORE HOUR

Okra is one of my favorite plants to grow. It looks quite exotic, with fingers of okra reaching toward the sun. Wherever you get your fresh okra, pick smallish pods, if you have a choice. Keeping the pods whole avoids the slimy quality that gives okra a bad reputation.

Vegetable oil spray

1 pound (455 g) whole okra pods

2 tablespoons (30 ml) bacon drippings or vegetable oil

1 large onion, halved and sliced in thin half-moons

1 can (15 ounces, or 425 g) crushed tomatoes with puree

1 can (10 ounces, or 280 g) tomatoes and green chiles, such as Ro-Tel

1 teaspoon kosher salt or coarse sea salt, or more to taste

1 teaspoon coarsely ground black pepper

① Generously spray the inside of the slow cooker with oil.

② Place the okra in the slow cooker.

③ Warm the bacon drippings in a medium skillet over medium heat. Add the onion and cook until limp, about 5 minutes. Scrape the mixture into the slow cooker. Add the tomatoes, tomatoes and green chiles, 1 teaspoon of salt, and the pepper. Cover and cook on the low heat setting for 3½ to 4 hours, until the okra is tender. Add more salt if you wish.

④ Serve the okra hot with some of the tomato and onion mixture. Yum.

EAST TEXAS LONG-COOKED GREEN BEANS

YIELD: SERVES 4 TO 6 | COOKING TIME: 3½ TO 4 HOURS ON LOW, CAN BE HELD ON WARM FOR 1 MORE HOUR

I have a Texas cookbook from more than 100 years ago that insisted fresh beans needed cooking for three to four hours. Well, here's a way to do that and not boil them totally to mush. They will, however, have that soft melting texture that made your great-grandmother's beans so satisfying. The black pepper adds real spark, so use it generously. If you have a few extra minutes, fry up two of the bacon slices initially, and add them, chopped, and their rendered fat to the beans. The browned bacon will add a slightly deeper flavor to the beans.

Vegetable oil spray

2 pounds (905 g) green beans, trimmed

1 medium onion, chopped fine

4 thick-cut bacon slices

2 teaspoons (4 g) coarse-ground black pepper, or more to taste

1 teaspoon kosher salt or coarse sea salt, or more to taste

½ teaspoon granulated sugar

2 cups (470 ml) chicken broth, preferably low-sodium

① Generously spray the inside of the slow cooker with oil.

② If you have the patience for it, cut the beans into 1- to 2-inch (2.5- to 5-cm) lengths. Place the remaining ingredients in the slow cooker. Cover and cook on the low heat setting for 3½ to 4 hours, until very tender.

③ Discard bacon slices, and add more pepper and salt, if you wish. Serve.

CORNBREAD WAS A MAINSTAY OF THE TEXAS DIET IN THE PIONEER ERA. NOT EVERYONE APPROVED, HOWEVER. ONE ENGLISH VISITOR CALLED IT "A MODIFICATION OF SAWDUST," AND ANOTHER TRAVELER RAILED AGAINST HAVING TO STAY IN "THE USUAL CORNBREAD-AND-COFFEE SORT OF HOTEL."

JALAPEÑO CORNBREAD WITH SORGHUM BUTTER

YIELD: SERVES 6 OR MORE | COOKING TIME: 2½ TO 3 HOURS ON HIGH

I took a cooking class many years ago from an East Texas chef named Lamoreaux who made a cakey irresistible cornbread that became the model for this. You can kiss dry cornbread goodbye when you prepare it in a slow cooker. I use Lamb's stone-ground yellow or white cornmeal from the family's Converse mill, a stone's throw from San Antonio. When time permits, I like the additional touch of sorghum butter, a traditional Texas grain crop that makes a molasses-like syrup. The sorghum butter is good on pancakes and biscuits, too.

CORNBREAD

1 cup plus 2 tablespoons (158 g) stone-ground cornmeal

⅔ cup (83 g) unbleached all-purpose flour

2 teaspoons (9 g) baking powder

1 teaspoon salt

¾ cup (1½ sticks, or 55 g) unsalted butter, softened

¼ cup (60 g) packed brown sugar

3 large eggs

½ cup (120 ml) buttermilk

1 cup (164 g) corn kernels, fresh or frozen

2 to 3 fresh jalapeños, minced

6 ounces (168 g) mild or medium Cheddar, grated (about 1½ cups)

SORGHUM BUTTER

4 ounces (1 stick, or 112 g) unsalted butter

3 tablespoons (60 g) sorghum or dark molasses

① Generously grease the inside of the slow cooker with butter.

② Pour ½ inch (1 cm) of water into the slow cooker. Arrange a 3-inch (7.5-cm) biscuit cutter in the middle of the cooker, if you have it. Otherwise, roll up an 18-inch (45-cm) piece of aluminum foil from one of its long sides into a snake. Then bend it into a coil to fit in the bottom of the slow cooker. Place this aluminum foil "rack" in the bottom of the slow cooker. The water should be below the level of the rack. Butter the inside of a quart (946 ml) soufflé dish or deep 6-inch (15-cm) cake pan.

③ In a small bowl, stir together the cornmeal, flour, baking powder, and salt. With a whisk or an electric mixer, whisk together the butter and brown sugar in another larger bowl, until the mixture is creamy and the sugar is mostly dissolved. Add the eggs, one at a time, then the buttermilk, corn kernels, jalapeños, and cheese. Add the dry ingredients to the wet ingredients, beating just a few strokes until the dry ingredients are incorporated.

④ Pour the batter into the prepared dish and transfer it to the slow cooker. Cover and cook on the low heat setting for 2½ to 3 hours, until a toothpick or cake tester inserted in the center comes out clean. If the cornbread seems underdone after 3 hours, leave off the slow cooker lid and cook for another 5 to 10 minutes, and check again.

⑤ While the cornbread cooks, make the sorghum butter. Whip it, whip it good—or at least whisk it well—in a small bowl until thoroughly combined. Reserve at room temperature.

⑥ When the cornbread is done, set the pan on a baking rack to cool. Cut the cornbread into wedges or squares. Serve with the sorghum butter.

DESSERTS AND
OTHER SWEETS

PEACH COBBLER

YIELD: SERVES 8 | COOKING TIME: 3 TO 3½ HOURS ON HIGH

Perhaps the most Texan of Texas desserts, cobbler is at its best when made with sweet summer peaches, maybe from Gillespie County, which wraps around such Hill Country towns as Fredericksburg, Stonewall, and Luckenbach. East Texas has its share of fine peaches, too, but they don't get the hype of those in the more traveled region of central Texas. If you are shopping for fresh peaches, clingstones generally ripen first, but they are best for pickling and canning. Look for freestone varieties to make the best cobbler. The greater cobbler world contains multitudes of topping styles, from pie crust to drop biscuits to this more cakey style, which my husband always insisted upon. The batter rises up through the filling and develops some crunchy edges in the process. The addition of a handful of slivered almonds enhances the crunch without calling attention to itself. Top with some Blue Bell Homemade Vanilla Ice Cream, the pride of Brenham, Texas.

1 stick (½ cup, or 112 g) unsalted butter

FILLING

2 pounds (about 8 medium, or 905 g) ripe juicy peaches, peeled, pitted, and sliced thickly, or thawed frozen peaches

¼ cup plus 2 tablespoons (150 g) turbinado sugar

1 tablespoon (15 ml) fresh lemon juice

BATTER

1¼ cups (157 g) unbleached all-purpose flour

½ cup plus 2 tablespoons (250 g) turbinado sugar

1 teaspoon ground cinnamon

½ teaspoon ground nutmeg

1 teaspoon baking powder

½ teaspoon baking soda

Pinch of salt

¾ cup plus 2 tablespoons (200 ml) buttermilk

1 teaspoon pure vanilla extract

Vanilla or caramel ice cream or softly whipped cream, optional

① Cut the stick of butter in 4 equal pieces and place in the slow cooker, turned to the high heat setting. Cover to melt butter, 15 to 20 minutes.

② Stir the filling ingredients together in a bowl.

③ Prepare the batter. In a medium bowl, stir together the flour, sugar, cinnamon, nutmeg, baking powder, baking soda, and salt. Mix in the buttermilk and vanilla. Spoon the batter over the butter in the slow cooker. Don't worry if you have a few holes or a bit of unevenness. (Don't stir the batter, which would make it turn out with fewer of the desirable crunchy edges.) Spoon the peach filling over the batter, arranging it so that there are more peaches around the outer edges of the slow cooker, rather than in the center. Cover and cook the cobbler for 3 to 3½ hours on the high heat setting, until the crust has oozed up through the fruit and is golden brown, lightly raised, and still moist.

④ Serve the cobbler warm, accompanied by ice cream or whipped cream, if you wish.

SPANISH SETTLERS BROUGHT PEACHES TO TEXAS IN THE SIXTEENTH CENTURY, WHEN THEY PLANTED TREES AT THEIR MISSIONS. TODAY, TEXAS IS ONE OF THE LEADING PEACH PRODUCERS IN THE UNITED STATES, HARVESTING ABOUT TWENTY MILLION POUNDS OF FRUIT EACH YEAR.

SUMMER PEACH AND BRAZOS BERRY CRISP

YIELD: SERVES 6 OR MORE | COOKING TIME: 3½ TO 4 HOURS ON LOW

You can never have too many peach desserts, given their quality, and they typically ripen around the time of berry picking, too. This crisp goes directly into the cooker, rather than in another dish with a water bath. The crunchy elements in the topping stay crisp, but the fruit and butter melt down into succulence. It won't brown much as it cooks so the pecans, brown sugar, and liberal dusting of cinnamon help it have a burnished appearance. If you have an oval slow cooker, use it for this for the optimum depth of the peaches and topping.

Unsalted butter

2 pounds (905 g) ripe juicy peaches, peeled, pitted, and sliced thickly, or unthawed frozen peaches

1 pint fresh raspberries, blackberries, dewberries, blueberries, or stemmed small strawberries

2 tablespoons (26 g) granulated sugar

TOPPING

1 cup (108 g) oats (the "old-fashioned" variety)

1 cup (110 g) chopped pecans

1 cup (225 g) packed brown sugar, preferably dark brown

1 cup (125 g) unbleached all-purpose flour

1 teaspoon ground cinnamon, plus more for the top

Pinch of salt

½ cup (1 stick) plus 2 tablespoons (140 g) unsalted butter

① Generously grease the inside of the slow cooker with butter.

② Dump the peaches, berries, and sugar in the slow cooker, and give a light stir.

③ Prepare the topping. Combine the oats, pecans, brown sugar, flour, cinnamon, and salt in a food processor until you have a coarse meal. Add the butter and pulse a few times until the mixture becomes evenly crumbly. Add the mixture to the slow cooker. Cover and cook on the low heat setting for 3½ to 4 hours.

④ Scoop out and serve warm. Leftovers are good at room temperature or reheated.

HEATHER'S CHOCOLATE-TOFFEE BROWNIES

YIELD: SERVES 6 OR MORE | COOKING TIME: 2½ TO 3 HOURS ON HIGH

Many people are surprised to know that all kinds of baked desserts come out better in the low moist environment of a slow cooker than in a more conventional oven. Brownies, cheesecakes, anything you want to have certain yummy gooiness to it. These brownies are Texas-over-the-top, a recipe I came up with back when my stepdaughter was a college student at Texas Woman's University. As with most of the "baked" desserts here, this one should be cooked on high.

Vegetable oil spray

6 tablespoons (84 g) unsalted butter

2 ounces (55 g) unsweetened chocolate

1 teaspoon pure vanilla extract

1 large egg and 1 large egg yolk

1 cup (200 g) granulated sugar

2 tablespoons (10 g) cocoa powder

½ cup (64 g) unbleached all-purpose flour

¾ cup (156 g) Skor toffee bits, or chopped chocolate-toffee bars

½ cup (55 g) pecan pieces, toasted in a dry skillet until fragrant

① Pour ½ inch (1 cm) of water into the slow cooker. To hold the baking pan above the water, place a 3-inch (7.5-cm) round biscuit cutter in the center of the slow cooker. Otherwise, roll up an 18-inch (45-cm) piece of aluminum foil from one of its long sides into a snake. Then bend it into a coil to fit in the bottom of the slow cooker. Place this aluminum foil rack in the bottom of the slow cooker. The water should be below the level of the rack. Spray the inside of a 6-inch (15-cm) springform pan with oil.

② Combine in a heavy medium saucepan the butter and unsweetened chocolate over medium-low heat. When melted together, remove from the heat and stir in the vanilla and the egg and yolk, mixing well. Stir in the sugar, cocoa, and flour just to combine. Avoid over-mixing. Stir in the toffee bits, just to combine. Pour batter into the prepared springform pan. Sprinkle pecans over the top.

③ Place the springform pan on the rack inside the slow cooker. Cover and cook on the high heat setting for 2½ to 3 hours. If the brownies still seem underdone, leave off the slow cooker lid and cook for another 5 to 10 minutes and check again. Do not overbake. The brownies will still look a little loose in the center when actually done.

④ Set the springform pan on a baking rack to cool. When cool, run a knife around the pan's inside edge and remove the side of the pan. Cut the brownies into wedges or squares in the size you wish. Enjoy.

BUTTERSCOTCH BLONDIES

YIELD: SERVES 6 OR MORE | COOKING TIME: 2½ TO 3 HOURS ON HIGH

When I first came across butterscotch brownies or "blondies" at bake sales, my reaction was puzzled. If they're brownies without the chocolate, then what's the point? It took me a little longer to wise up to the fact that butterscotch is one of the best flavors ever, so who needs chocolate? As with the brownies in this chapter, the lower moist heat of the slow cooker helps set the deliciously gooey texture.

Vegetable oil spray

1½ cups (64 g) unbleached all-purpose flour

1½ teaspoons baking powder

½ teaspoon salt

1 cup (225 g) unsalted butter, softened

1½ cups (115 g) packed brown sugar, preferably dark brown

1 tablespoon molasses or cane syrup

2 large eggs

1 teaspoon pure vanilla extract

¾ cup (83 g) chopped pecans

① Pour ½ inch (1 cm) of water into the slow cooker. To hold the baking pan above the water, place a 3-inch (7.5-cm) round biscuit cutter in the center of the slow cooker. Otherwise, roll up an 18-inch (45-cm) piece of aluminum foil from one of its long sides into a snake. Then bend it into a coil to fit in the bottom of the slow cooker. Place this aluminum foil rack in the bottom of the slow cooker. The water should be below the level of the rack. Spray the inside of a 6-inch (15-cm) springform pan with oil.

② Stir together the flour, baking powder, and salt.

③ With an electric mixer on high speed, beat the daylights out of the butter and brown sugar, until the mixture is fluffy, then add the molasses and continue beating on medium speed until well incorporated. Mix in the eggs one at a time, beating until each is blended, then beat in the vanilla. On low speed, add about one-half of the flour mixture, then add the rest as the first flour disappears into the mixture. Beat just until the flour is blended, stopping if needed to scrape down the sides of the bowl. Stir in the pecans. Spread the batter (it will be thick) in the pan, smoothing the surface.

④ Place the springform pan on the rack inside the slow cooker. Cover and cook on the high heat setting for 2½ to 3 hours. If the blondies still seem underdone, leave off the slow cooker lid and cook for another 5 to 10 minutes and check again. Do not overbake. The blondies will still look a little loose in the center when actually done.

⑤ Set the springform pan on a baking rack to cool. When cool, run a knife around the pan's inside edge and remove the side of the pan. Cut the blondies into wedges or squares in the size you wish, and serve.

RIO STAR GRAPEFRUIT PUDDING CAKE

YIELD: SERVES 6 | COOKING TIME: 1½ TO 2 HOURS ON HIGH

The prime season for the Rio Grande Valley's grapefruit coincides with Christmas. Almost two decades ago, a friend living in McAllen shipped us a box of hefty grapefruit as a holiday gift. They were so much better than what could be found in grocery stores at the time that we began to order them every year, from November through the season's April conclusion. The juice makes a sprightly pudding cake, with a delicate layer of cake on top and the citrusy pudding below. Grapefruit peel and a touch of citrus oil boosts the flavor in a welcome way. It's not common to find grapefruit oil though, so I call for lemon or orange. The few drops add citrusy character without confusing the grapefruit's taste.

Unsalted butter

1 cup (200 g) granulated sugar

¼ cup (32 g) unbleached all-purpose flour

¼ teaspoon salt

1 cup (235 ml) buttermilk

2 teaspoons (4 g) grated grapefruit zest and ⅓ cup (80 ml) fresh-squeezed Rio Star grapefruit juice or other red or pink grapefruit juice (about ½ grapefruit)

2 to 3 drops lemon or orange oil

3 large eggs, separated, and yolks whisked together

¼ teaspoon cream of tartar

Fresh mint sprigs for garnish, optional

1. Generously grease the inside of the slow cooker with butter.

2. Stir together in a large bowl the sugar, flour, and salt, then stir in the buttermilk, then the grapefruit zest and juice, lemon oil, and then the whisked egg yolks.

3. Beat the egg whites with an electric mixer until foamy, then add the cream of tartar, and continue to beat until the egg whites form stiff peaks. Fold the egg whites into the cake batter, about one-third at a time. Add the next batch when you have just a few streaks of the previous egg white visible.

4. Pour the batter into the slow cooker and cover. Cook on the high heat setting for 1½ to 2 hours, until the cake has just begun to brown and pull away from the slow cooker at the edges, and the top is lightly puffed and holds its shape. Uncover and let the cake sit for at least 15 minutes before serving warm, at room temperature, or chilled. Scoop up from the bottom to get some of the pudding from below as well as the cakey top. (The colder the cake, the thicker the pudding will be.) Serve in bowls garnished, if you wish, with mint.

THE WARM MOIST
ENVIRONMENT OF
THE SLOW COOKER
MAKES IT A FLAWLESS
CONTAINER
FOR BAKING A
CHEESECAKE TO
A CREAMY, DREAMY
PERFECTION—
WITH NO CRACKS
IN THE CAKE.

MARGARITA CHEESECAKE

YIELD: SERVES 8 | COOKING TIME: 2 TO 2½ HOURS ON HIGH

If you've ever feared making a cheesecake because of its persnickety potential for cracking, here is the solution for you. The warm moist environment of the slow cooker makes it the flawless container for baking a cake to creamy perfection. From the crust up, this one blends the flavors of the state's favorite adult thirst-quencher.

CRUST

2 packed cups pretzel sticks

2 tablespoons (26 g) granulated sugar

3 tablespoons (42 g) unsalted butter, melted

CHEESECAKE

19 ounces (535 g) cream cheese (two 8-ounce packages and one 3-ounce package), softened

½ cup (115 g) sour cream

½ cup plus 2 tablespoons (126 g) granulated sugar

¾ teaspoon salt

3 large eggs, at room temperature

3 tablespoons (45 ml) Triple Sec or other orange liqueur

2 tablespoons (30 ml) tequila, preferably silver

1 tablespoon (6 g) grated lime zest (from about 1 large lime) and 2 tablespoons (30 ml) lime juice

① Pour ½ inch of water into the slow cooker. To hold the baking pan above the water, place a 3-inch (7.5-cm) round biscuit cutter in the center of the slow cooker. Otherwise, roll up an 18-inch (45-cm) piece of aluminum foil from one of its long sides into a coil and fit it in the bottom of the slow cooker. The water should be below the level of the coil.

② With a food processor, zap the pretzels with the sugar until you have crumbs. Pour in the butter and pulse several times to incorporate. Scrape crumb mixture into a 6-inch (15-cm) springform pan and press into an even layer with the bowl of a spoon. Rinse out the food processor work bowl and return it to the processor.

③ Combine the cream cheese, sour cream, sugar, and salt in the food processor, and pulse a few times until combined and smooth. Add eggs, Triple Sec, tequila, and lime zest and juice, and pulse several times just to combine.

④ Scrape filling into buttered pan and smooth top. Place the pan on the rack in the slow cooker and cover. Cook on high for 2 to 2½ hours, until cake is lightly set but is still moist looking, and the internal temperature is approximately 160°F (71°C) on an instant-read thermometer. Turn off the slow cooker and let cheesecake sit in it covered for 1 to 1½ hours. Transfer to baking rack.

⑤ Let the cheesecake cool to room temperature. Cover and refrigerate until well-chilled and set, at least 4 hours and up to 2 days.

⑥ Shortly before serving, run a small knife around inside edge of pan, then remove the side of pan carefully. Cut into slices, cleaning knife blade off with hot water between cuts.

CHEESECAKE WITH PRICKLY PEAR SYRUP

YIELD: SERVES 8 | COOKING TIME: 1¾ TO 2 HOURS ON HIGH

As with the previous recipe, the warm moist environment of the slow cooker makes it an exceptional way to prepare a cheesecake. The cake and crust are more traditional here, providing a simple canvas for a final flourish of electric magenta syrup made from the fruit of the prickly pear cactus.

CRUST

1¼ cups (105 g) graham cracker crumbs

1 tablespoon (13 g) granulated sugar

3 tablespoons (42 g) unsalted butter, melted

CHEESECAKE

19 ounces (535 g) cream cheese (two 8-ounce packages and one 3-ounce package), softened

¾ cup (150 g) granulated sugar

½ teaspoon salt

⅓ cup (77 g) sour cream

2 large eggs, at room temperature

2 teaspoons (4 g) grated lemon zest

1 teaspoon pure vanilla extract

Prickly pear syrup, such as Cherie's

① Pour ½ inch (1 cm) of water into the slow cooker. To hold the baking pan above the water, place a 3-inch (7.5-cm) round biscuit cutter in the center of the slow cooker. Otherwise, roll up an 18-inch (45-cm) piece of aluminum foil from one of its long sides into a snake. Then bend it into a coil to fit in the bottom of the slow cooker. Place this aluminum foil rack in the bottom of the slow cooker. The water should be below the level of the rack.

② Stir together crumbs and granulated sugar in bowl, then stir in the butter until evenly moistened. Pour crumb mixture into 6-inch (15-cm) springform pan and press into an even layer with the bowl of a spoon.

③ Combine cream cheese, granulated sugar, and salt in food processor, and process until combined and smooth. Add sour cream, eggs, lemon zest, and vanilla, and pulse several times just to combine.

④ Scrape filling into buttered pan and smooth top. Place the pan on the rack in the slow cooker and cover. Cook on high for 1¾ to 2½ hours, until cake is lightly set but is still moist looking, and the internal temperature is approximately 160°F (71°C) on an instant-read thermometer. Turn off the slow cooker and let cheesecake sit in it covered for 1 to 1½ hours. Transfer to baking rack.

⑤ Let the cheesecake cool to room temperature. Cover and refrigerate until well-chilled and set, at least 4 hours and up to 2 days.

⑥ Shortly before serving, run a small knife around inside edge of pan, then remove the side of pan carefully. Cut into slices, cleaning knife blade off with hot water between cuts. Drizzle a couple of spoonfuls of prickly pear syrup over each slice before serving.

PRALINE BREAD PUDDING

YIELD: SERVES 8 | COOKING TIME: 2¾ TO 3¼ HOURS ON HIGH

I love driving by pecan orchards or "bottoms" in any season. The trees are so pretty when leafed out and later when heavy with nuts. I might admire them most in winter, when the dark branches look so stark against a gray sky. The native Texas nut adds an important element of crunch to this bread pudding, blending with vanilla, brown sugar, and spice, to make all things nice. The bourbon-laced sauce isn't a necessity, except in our family.

BREAD PUDDING

½ cup (75 g) dark raisins

⅓ cup (80 ml) bourbon or other whiskey

6 to 7 cups (210 to 245 g) lightly packed bite-size cubes day-old French or Italian-style bread

½ cup (55 g) chopped pecans

4 large eggs

2½ cups (570 ml) half-and-half

½ cup (115 g) packed brown sugar

½ cup (100 g) granulated sugar

½ stick (¼ cup, or 55 g) unsalted butter, melted

1 tablespoon (15 ml) pure vanilla extract

½ teaspoon ground cinnamon

¼ teaspoon ground nutmeg

WHISKEY SAUCE

1 stick (½ cup, or 55 g) unsalted butter

1½ cups (180 g) confectioner's sugar

2 egg yolks, lightly whisked

¼ cup plus 2 tablespoons (88 ml) bourbon or other whiskey

① Generously grease the inside of the slow cooker with butter.

② Combine the raisins and whiskey in a small bowl.

③ Arrange the bread in the bottom of the slow cooker and scatter the pecans over it. When the raisins have absorbed most of the whiskey, scatter them and any remaining whiskey over the bread. Whisk together the eggs, half-and-half, both sugars, butter, vanilla, cinnamon, and nutmeg, and pour the custard mixture evenly over the bread. Lightly pat the bread down into the custard. Let the mixture sit at room temperature about 15 minutes, then stir and pat back down again. A bit of the bread should remain just above the custard.

④ Cover and cook the pudding on the high heat setting for 2½ to 3 hours, until the pudding is slightly poofed and golden. Remove the lid and cook for another 15 to 20 minutes, for some of the moisture to evaporate.

⑤ While the pudding bakes, prepare the sauce. Combine the butter and sugar in a medium saucepan. Warm over medium heat until the butter and sugar melt together. Stir two tablespoons of the butter-sugar mixture into the egg yolks, then pour it back into the rest of the butter-sugar mixture and whisk until combined, about another minute. Remove from the heat and immediately whisk in the whiskey. The sauce will be somewhat thin, but it thickens as it cools.

⑥ Serve the pudding warm, spooned onto individual plates, with a few tablespoons of the sauce poured over each. Pass the remaining sauce separately.

CHOCOLATE "SHEET" CAKE

YIELD: SERVES 8 OR MORE | COOKING TIME: 2 TO 2½ HOURS ON HIGH

Found at every bake sale and potluck and quite a few birthdays, Texas sheet or sheath cake shares some similarities to the more complicated and equally popular German chocolate cake. Usually a simple, one-bowl, one-layer, sheet cake has an easy icing too. The cake typically includes a couple of traditional Texas ingredients—buttermilk and pecans—but it is thought to have the Texas name bestowed on it because of its usually hefty size. This slow-cooker version lost its "big as Texas" sheet pan look but gained extra moistness, even with a reduction in the standard amount of butter. I like to add a little cayenne for an elusive zip, but you can leave it out, if you wish. The dead-simple icing, or sheathing in olden-day terms, is poured over the cake while both are warm.

CAKE

¾ cup (165 g) unsalted butter

½ cup plus 1 tablespoon (48 g) cocoa powder

1 cup (235 ml) buttermilk or yogurt

½ cup (120 ml) water

2 teaspoons (10 ml) pure vanilla extract

2 cups (250 g) unbleached all-purpose flour

1¾ cup (350 g) granulated sugar

1 teaspoon baking powder

¼ teaspoon salt

¼ teaspoon ground cayenne, optional

ICING

¼ cup (55 g) unsalted butter

2 tablespoons (10 g) cocoa powder

1½ to 2 tablespoons (7 to 28 ml) half-and-half or whole milk

½ teaspoon pure vanilla extract

1 cup (120 g) confectioner's sugar

Pinch of salt

⅔ cup (73 g) chopped pecans

① Pour ½ inch (1 cm) of water into a 5- to 6-quart (4.7 to 5.7-l) slow cooker. An oval one works particularly well for this. To hold the baking pan above the water, place a 3-inch (7.5-cm) round biscuit cutter in the center of the slow cooker. Otherwise, roll up an 18-inch (45-cm) piece of aluminum foil, from one of its long sides, into a snake. Then bend the foil into a coil to fit in the bottom of the slow cooker. Place this aluminum foil rack in the bottom of the slow cooker. The water should be below the level of the rack. Butter a high-sided 6- or 7-inch (15- to 17.5-cm) round cake pan.

② Melt the butter in a large heavy saucepan over medium heat. Remove the pan from the heat. Stir in the cocoa with a flat whisk or large spoon, eliminating all lumps. Mix in the buttermilk, water, and vanilla. Stir together the flour, sugar, baking powder, salt, and optional cayenne. Mix them into the chocolate mixture.

③ Pour batter into the prepared cake pan. Set the cake pan in the slow cooker. Cover and cook on high for 2 to 2½ hours, until a toothpick inserted into the center comes out clean. Turn off the slow cooker and let the cake sit in it for about 30 more minutes.

④ While the cake is still sitting in the slow cooker, prepare the icing. Melt the butter with the cocoa in a saucepan over medium heat. Add the half-and-half, and heat mixture through. Stir in the remaining ingredients.

⑤ Run a thin knife around the cake and turn out onto a baking rack. Spoon the warm icing over the warm cake. Slice into wedges to serve right away, or cool to room temperature before cutting.

THIS SLOW COOKER VERSION LACKS THE 'BIG AS TEXAS' LOOK OF A TRUE SHEET CAKE, BUT IT GAINS EXTRA MOISTNESS EVEN WITH A REDUCTION IN THE STANDARD AMOUNT OF BUTTER.

PEAR BUTTER

YIELD: MAKES APPROXIMATELY 6 CUPS (3 PINTS OR 1.4 L) | COOKING TIME: 6 TO 7 HOURS ON HIGH, 10 TO 11 HOURS ON LOW

Kieffer pears, a crisp somewhat coarse-textured pear, are sought after by discriminating cooks for making butter or sauce. A friend's grandmother would never make her pear butter with anything else. Kieffer pears never caught on commercially, probably because they aren't all that special for eating out of hand. You see them around old farmhouses and barns in central and eastern parts of the state. Use Bartlett or Anjou pears if you have no Kieffers. If you wish, replace a few of the pears with apples. Enjoy some of the pear butter warm on toast or biscuits, or add some over your breakfast yogurt. The rest can be frozen or refrigerated for later use.

Vegetable oil spray

5 pounds (2.3 kg) pears (about 10), peeled, quartered, and cored

1 cup (200 g) granulated sugar

¾ cup (170 g) packed dark brown sugar

1 tablespoon (15 ml) fresh lemon juice

¾ teaspoon salt

2 cinnamon sticks

① Generously spray the inside of the slow cooker with oil.

② In a food processor with the grater blade, shred the pear sections, in several batches. Scrape pears into the slow cooker. Stir in the granulated sugar, brown sugar, lemon juice, salt, and cinnamon sticks. Cover and cook on high for 6 to 7 hours, or low for 10 to 11 hours, until thick and medium to deep brown.

③ Remove the cinnamon sticks. Cool the pear butter. Spoon into freezer containers and freeze for up to several months, or spoon into jars and refrigerate for up to about 1 month.

FIG PRESERVES

YIELD: MAKES APPROXIMATELY 6 CUPS (3 PINTS) | COOKING TIME: 4 TO 5 HOURS ON HIGH, 8 TO 9 HOURS ON LOW

My husband and his siblings spent many a happy summer visiting their grandmother's Victorian-era home well outside of Austin in what was then Sprinkle, Texas. Bill always remembered feasting on plump fresh figs as well as spooning and eating his grandmother's fig preserves right out of the canning jar. These days, Sprinkle is actually a part of northeast Austin, and the old homestead is known far and wide as the Barr Mansion, a lovely center for weddings and other special events.

Vegetable oil spray

3 pounds (1.4 kg) fresh figs, stemmed and halved, or quartered if especially plump

3 cups (600 g) granulated sugar

1 teaspoon dried ginger

1 cup (235 ml) water

1 thin-skinned lemon, sliced thin and any seeds removed

1 tablespoon (15 ml) fresh lemon juice

① Spray the inside of the slow cooker generously with oil.

② Combine all of the ingredients in the slow cooker. Cover and cook on the high heat setting for 4 to 5 hours or on low for 8 to 9 hours. If possible, stir the mixture up about halfway through the cooking time on high or twice at equal intervals on low. It's not essential if you are not present, but the preserves will cook most evenly this way.

③ The preserves are ready when the mixture is thick and chunky but will still drop easily off of a spoon. (Preserves will thicken when cool.) Spoon into jars to refrigerate, or into freezer containers and freeze for up to several months.

FLAN MAKES THE
QUINTESSENTIAL
FLOURISH AFTER
A TEX-MEX MEAL.
MY VERSION
SUPPLEMENTS
THE SILKINESS
OF THE FLAN
WITH FRAGRANT
UNDERTONES OF
VANILLA AND
ALMOND.

FLAN

YIELD: SERVES 8 | COOKING TIME: 2 TO 2½ HOURS ON HIGH

Flan makes the quintessential flourish after a Tex-Mex meal. The version I remember opening my eyes to its possibilities was served at Ninfa's in Houston. It was back in the day when there were just a couple of restaurants and they were overseen by founder Ninfa Rodriguez Laurenzo herself. Here's my own version, one that supplements the silkiness of the flan with fragrant undertones of vanilla and almond.

½ cup (100 g) granulated sugar

1 can (14 ounces, or 414 ml) sweetened condensed milk

2 cups (470 ml) whole milk

3 large eggs

4 large egg yolks

1 tablespoon (15 ml) pure vanilla extract

2 teaspoons (10 ml) almond extract

1. Scatter sugar in a 2-inch-deep (5-cm) 6-inch (15-cm) cake pan. Place the pan over a stove burner and turn heat to medium. Using oven mitts, caramelize the sugar in the pan, shaking the pan as needed to turn sugar a rich medium-brown. Set aside to cool.

2. Pour ½ inch (1 cm) of water into the slow cooker. To hold the baking pan above the water, place a 3-inch (7.5-cm) round biscuit cutter in the center of the slow cooker. Otherwise, roll up an 18-inch (45-cm) piece of aluminum foil from one of its long sides into a snake. Then bend it into a coil to fit in the bottom of the slow cooker. Place this aluminum foil rack in the bottom of the slow cooker. The water should be below the level of the rack.

3. With an electric mixer, beat together the condensed milk, whole milk, eggs, yolks, and vanilla and almond extracts just until combined. Pour the custard mixture into the cooled pan of caramel. Transfer the pan to the slow cooker. Cover and cook on the high heat setting for 2 to 2½ hours.

4. Let the flan cool for an additional hour in the slow cooker, then remove the pan from the cooker, cover it, and refrigerate for at least 4 hours and up to overnight.

5. To unmold the chilled flan, run a knife between the edge of the flan and pan. Invert onto a plate and serve.

ACKNOWLEDGMENTS

I wasn't supposed to author this book on my own. Life, and death, got in the way. My forever collaborator and coauthor, husband Bill Jamison, died of cancer after we had signed the contract, but before we had the opportunity to dig into the project. I must thank the most supportive network of friends, family, and colleagues anyone has ever been blessed with. You helped me move forward, and to know that this was the place to start.

Thank you Bruce Shaw, founder and publisher of Harvard Common Press, and Dan Rosenberg, editor-in-chief, for bringing me a project with a vision for something greater than it might sound on the surface. The Quarto Group became part of the publishing family during the book's writing, and I look forward to working with its team as well. Doe Coover, agent extraordinaire, gently nudged me forward at a time that I just wanted to stare at the wood grain in the kitchen cabinets. Friend and sometime editor, Harriet Bell, you guided me on the slow but sure path, too.

Once a Day Marketing wizards Jim Glover and Marianne Tenenbaum came into my life at just the right time to help me figure out how to honor the past, while moving ahead. America's Test Kitchen, through your *Slow Cooker Revolution*, you helped revolutionize my thinking about how to get dinner ready. Beth Hensberger, you gave me further inspiration. Cathy Barber and Deborah Durham, thanks for letting me pepper you with questions when I was feeling slow on the uptake. Molly Boyle and Mario Cervantes, you helped me more than you will know.

I have been fortunate to have a network of Texans from whom I have been able to draw culinary inspiration over many years, before and after I lived there. The seminal figures have probably been the Mueller BBQ family, cheese queen Paula Lambert, chef Stephan Pyles, steakhouse proprietors Tom and Lisa Perini, *Texas Monthly* food maven Patricia Sharpe, author Robb Walsh, culinary librarian Ann McGuffin Barton, market farmer Carol Ann Sayle, and a collection of fine folks from the Central Markets, starting at the top with Charles Butt.

My Austin family inspired what could be done in a slow cooker, to help a busy household put great meals on the table. Thank you, stepdaughter Heather Jamison Neale and husband JB Neale, and grandkids Riley, Bronwyn, and Chloe Neale. Nothing is better than cooking together and then sitting down with you for a meal. You fill me with joy.

After all that staring at the kitchen cabinets, I decided that a book with a Texas theme could honor Bill's heritage and the many good times we had throughout the state. It could also showcase some of our favorite homey foods. As the late great singer-songwriter Guy Clark exclaimed, " . . . ain't that Texas Cookin' something."

ABOUT THE AUTHOR

Cheryl Alters Jamison is the multiple-award-winning author or co-author of more than a dozen books on regional American cooking and on grilling and barbecue, including *Smoke & Spice*, *The Barbecue Lover's Big Book of BBQ Sauces*, *The Border Cookbook*, and *Texas Home Cooking*.

INDEX

If you love *Texas Slow Cooker*, you'll also love these other Harvard Common Press titles by Cheryl and Bill Jamison:

The Barbecue Lover's Big Book of BBQ Sauces: 225 Extraordinary Sauces, Rubs, Marinades, Mops, Bastes, Pastes, and Salsas, for Smoke-Cooking or Grilling
ISBN: 978-1-55832-845-7

The Barbecue Lover's Big Book of BBQ Sauces is the first and only barbecue sauce book that caters to how outdoor chefs really cook. The book features 225 recipes, along with full-color photography, for barbecue sauces, marinades, mops, pastes, dry rubs, and more, along with detailed instructions on using a recipe for smoking, grilling, or both.

Born to Grill: An American Celebration
ISBN: 978-1-55832-291-2

A collection of 300 sizzlingly satisfying all-American recipes guaranteed to release the inner griller in every backyard cook. This award-winning cooking team shows you how to create a tremendous variety of terrific grilled food, from hot burgers and haute dogs to serious steaks and sizzling seafood, from fired-up pizzas and crisp vegetables to finger lickin' good deserts.

Smoke & Spice, Updated and Expanded 3rd Edition: Cooking With Smoke, the Real Way to Barbecue
ISBN: 978-1-55832-836-5

The only authoritative book on the subject of genuine smoke-cooked barbecue. Outdoor cooking experts Cheryl and Bill Jamison have added 100 brand-new recipes, the very latest information on tools, fuels, equipment, and technique, and loads more of their signature wit, charm, and reverence for BBQ.

Sublime Smoke: Bold New Flavors Inspired by the Old Art of Barbecue
ISBN: 978-1-55832-292-9

For everyone who savors the husky resonance and deep flavors of wood-smoked barbecue, *Sublime Smoke* features more than 200 recipes that amply demonstrate how creative and delicious smoke cooking can be. *Sublime Smoke* reveals both the versatility and the unbeatable goodness of smoke cooking.

Texas Home Cooking: 400 Terrific and Comforting Recipes Full of Big, Bright Flavors and Loads of Down-Home Goodness
ISBN: 978-1-55832-059-8

The definitive book on Texas cooking—which has been influenced by cuisines around the world, including Eastern Europe and Mexico—by distinguished food writers Cheryl and Bill Jamison, who traveled for two years around the state talking with home cooks, chefs, barbecue experts, fishermen, and farmers.

100 Grilling Recipes You Can't Live Without: A Lifelong Companion
ISBN: 978-1-55832-801-3

For the folks that want the top recipes and mastery attainable for even the home cook, Cheryl and Bill Jamison lay the groundwork and roll out only the "best of" in *100 Grilling Recipes You Can't Live Without*. This backyard essential delivers championship recipes with the Jamison's signature lively wit that reinvigorates the endless utility of this popular cooking technique.